Josiah Tyler

Forty Years Among The Zulus

Josiah Tyler

Forty Years Among The Zulus

ISBN/EAN: 9783742810540

Manufactured in Europe, USA, Canada, Australia, Japa

Cover: Foto ©ninafisch / pixelio.de

Manufactured and distributed by brebook publishing software (www.brebook.com)

Josiah Tyler

Forty Years Among The Zulus

FORTY YEARS AMONG THE ZULUS

BY

REV. JOSIAH TYLER

MISSIONARY OF THE A. B. C. F. M.

BOSTON AND CHICAGO
Congregational Sunday-School and Publishing Society

COPYRIGHT, 1891, BY
CONGREGATIONAL SUNDAY-SCHOOL AND PUBLISHING SOCIETY.

TO THE MEMORY OF

MY BELOVED WIFE,

WHO FOR

THIRTY-EIGHT YEARS LABORED UNWEARIEDLY

FOR THE EVANGELIZATION OF

THE ZULUS,

AND WAS THEN CALLED TO HIGHER SERVICE.

NOTE.

RELUCTANTLY obliged by ill health to relinquish mission work in Africa, it has been suggested that I publish some account of the beginning and growth of the evangelization of the Zulus. Thanks are due to the editors of The New York Observer and other papers for permission to make use of articles which have occasionally appeared from my pen while in Natal. If what I have written shall lead any one to consecrate himself to the work of the Master in South Africa, I shall be fully repaid. J. T.

INTRODUCTION.

IT is good to observe a people through the eyes of one who has long lived *among* them and *for* them. The unselfish soul is the best observer. He sees truthfully who sees the good, that he may enlarge it; the evil, that he may cure it. For a study of races, the devotion of love is the light of wisdom. For this reason the observations and reflections of this book will have a just and permanent value.

The "heroes of the Dark Continent" are not all named in the records of explorations and discoveries. The worth and courage of the missionary, who, by his fidelity in preaching and living the gospel, discovers the man in the savage, are less conspicuous but no less real. England may trace many streams of her power to the fountains that were opened by the teachers and preachers of Jesus when her ancestors were pagans. If another England — a "Greater Britain" — appear in South Africa, with commerce, education, a well-organized society, and the beneficent forces of religion, it will be created by the same truth and personal consecration. Missionary Tyler will not live to see the society of his hope, but when it comes and its history shall be written, the "Forty Years among the Zulus" will be named as among the seeds without which there could have been no harvest.

It is said that nearly one fourth of the native inhabitants of Africa are of the Bantu race, of which the Zulu is doubtless the most interesting tribe. This book makes evident that they are not only numerous, but have a capacity for great things. In their courage and respect for property rights is found the promise of a new nation. If Paul plant and Apollos water, God will give the increase. This book describes the people as they are: their vulgarities, superstitions, their somewhat offensive but vigorous naturalness, and proves what may be done with them by the power of the gospel. What we call civilization is now entering Africa. The Christian religion must go with it, or its selfish and depraving accompaniments — impurity, intemperance — will make the light of knowledge darker than the native ignorance.

There is a fascination in reading the chapters describing Zulu life as they follow one after another, because it is always interesting to read of human nature, and more than interesting to read a book in which an earnest soul describes the consistent devotion of all his working years. Mr. Tyler is the son of Bennet Tyler, D.D., of wide fame as a teacher and theologian. Inheriting much of his father's power, alluring opportunities of usefulness here were presented to him. But he was possessed of the spirit of a missionary and could be nothing else with a whole heart. There were no unconsecrated reserves in his nature. He was fitted for his work by a singularly active mind, a tender and yearning spirit, humor, common sense, and a heart loyal to Christ. He still calls the natives his people; and in his enforced absence, though with children and friends, really lives among the Zulus. "I see them every Sunday," he says, "and find myself in imagination preaching to them in their own language the wonderful truths of God's love."

C. M. LAMSON, D.D.

St. Johnsbury, Vt.

CONTENTS.

CHAPTER I.
LEAVING HOME.

Choice of the South African Mission. — Marriage and Ordination. — Leaving Home. — Stop at Cape Town. — Rev. Dr. Philip. — Sight of Natal. — Reception by Rev. Daniel Lindley. — Ride in an Ox-wagon 17

CHAPTER II.
STUDY OF THE LANGUAGE.

Rev. Newton Adams, M.D., and wife. — Study of the Language. — Mistakes in Speaking Zulu . . 29

CHAPTER III.
OUR MISSION STATION.

Going to my Station. — Mr. Lindley accompanies me. — Incidents in Mr. Lindley's Life. — View of Esidumbini. — Taking Possession. — Mrs. Lindley 35

CHAPTER IV.
LIFE IN A KRAAL.

Life in a Zulu Kraal. — How the Huts are made. — A Zulu Pantry. — Owner of the Kraal refuses to have a Door in his Hut. — Appeal to Ancestral Custom. — Winning the Confidence of the People 41

CHAPTER V.
HOUSE BUILDING.

In a Dilemma. — Rev. Aldin Grout. — His attempt to Teach a King his Letters. — An American Mail. — Mrs. Tyler's Feelings in view of the Work 48

CHAPTER VI.
ZULU DRESS.

Zulu Wardrobe. — Shaving the Head. — Head Ring. — Headdress of the Women and Young Men. — Fondness for Ornaments 57

CHAPTER VII.
DIFFICULTIES ENCOUNTERED.

Reply to the Question, "Who made you?" — The Great Spirit. — Ignorance. — Selfishness. — Need of Patience. — My "Better Half." — Zulu Consciences 63

CHAPTER VIII.
TOILING AND WAITING.

Mrs. Tyler's Retrospect. — Hulumene. — Dambusa. — Muscular Christianity. — Gravity Upset ... 68

CHAPTER IX.
WILD ANIMALS.

Buffaloes. — Umfulawe's Narrow Escape. — An Englishman's Adventure. — Lions. — Leopards. — Wild Dogs. — Baboons 73

CHAPTER X.
CROCODILES AND SNAKES.

Butler's Narrow Escape. — A Dutchman's Adventure. — Pythons. — Venomous Serpents. — Puff Adders. — The "Imamba." — Zulu Carrying a Serpent on his Head. — Snakes good Ratcatchers. — Effect of Tobacco on Serpents. — Remedies for Snake-bites 83

CHAPTER XI.
SPIRIT WORSHIP.

Doctors of Divination. — "Smellers Out." — Zulu Prayers. — Sacrifices 93

CHAPTER XII.
ZULU SUPERSTITIONS. 104

CHAPTER XIII.
POLYGAMY AND OTHER EVIL PRACTICES.
Chattelizing of Women. — Beer Drinking. — Smoking Wild Hemp 117

CHAPTER XIV.
ENCOURAGEMENTS.
Church Organized. — Prodigals Returning. — Dambusa again. — Experience of Young Converts. — Christianity must Precede Civilization 125

CHAPTER XV.
THE SABBATH AT ESIDUMBINI. 134

CHAPTER XVI.
VISIT TO THE UNITED STATES. — NEW WORK.
Trial of leaving Children on returning to Africa. — Location at Umsunduzi. — Visiting an Out-station. — Mrs. Tyler's Observations 140

CHAPTER XVII.
EXPERIENCES AT UMSUNDUZI. 149

CHAPTER XVIII.
ZULU CHURCHES.
Disciplinable Offenses in Zulu Churches. — Mission Rules. — Legislation of a Native Church. — Polygamous Converts. — One in a Dilemma . . 158

CHAPTER XIX.
ZULU CHRISTIANS.
Their Courage. — Faith. — Happy Deaths 163

CHAPTER XX.
ZULU PREACHERS.

Revs. James Dube and Ira Adams. — Umsingapansi. — Cases of Lapse. — Specimens of Zulu Addresses 171

CHAPTER XXI.
ZULU CUSTOMS AND LAWS.

Origin of the Name "Kaffir." — Similarity of Zulu and Jewish Customs. — Number of Zulus in Natal in 1843 and in 1889. — Regard for their Chiefs. — Independence. — Zulu Lad's Escape from Cannibals 181

CHAPTER XXII.
ZULU CHARACTERISTICS.

Physical Strength of the Zulus. — Politeness. — Love of Fun. — Skill in Debate. — Ingenuity. — Teachableness 188

CHAPTER XXIII.
ZULU WEDDINGS AND FUNERALS.

Cetywayo's Marrying his Fifteenth Wife. — Zulu Girls "Popping the Question." — Publicly Choosing a Husband. — Funeral Ceremonies . . 199

CHAPTER XXIV.
ZULU KINGS AND WARS.

Chaka, Dingaan, Umpande, Cetywayo. — Zulu War in 1869 and 1870. — Quarrel between Cetywayo and Usibepu. — Death of the Former. — Undinizulu. — Rebellion and Sentence 212

CHAPTER XXV.
ZULU FOLKLORE. 229

CHAPTER XXVI.
DECEASED AMERICAN MISSIONARIES.

Revs. Champion, Bryant, Marsh, McKinney and wife, Ireland, Abraham and wife, Wilder, Stone, Lloyd and wife, Robbins and wife, Döhne, Pinkerton, Butler, Mrs. Tyler 236

CHAPTER XXVII.
NATIVE EDUCATION.

Seminary at Adams. — "Jubilee Hall." — The Theological School. — "Inanda Seminary." — "Umzumbe Home." — Kraal Schools. — Government Aid. — Books in the Zulu Language 253

CHAPTER XXVIII.
THE MISSIONARY OUTLOOK.

Semi-Centennial. — Past and Present Laborers. — Condition of the Field. — E. C. A. M. — Other Societies. — Boer Farm Mission. — Trappists. — Missionary Outlook. — Need of Help 260

CHAPTER XXIX.
FACTS CONCERNING NATAL.

When Discovered. — Early History. — Elysium in South Africa. — Climate. — Cost of Living. — Cattle and Sheep Farming. — Pests. — Ticks and White Ants 269

CHAPTER XXX.
PHYSICAL FEATURES AND POLITICAL AFFAIRS.

Natal. — Durban.— Maritzburg.— Granite Caves. — Geological Features. — Coal Beds. — Flora Waterfalls. — Escape of a Dutchman. — Political Affairs. — Imports and Exports. — Railways. — Native Question 283

APPENDIX.

Later Missions. — The Zulu Language. — The Exiled Chiefs 295

FORTY YEARS AMONG THE ZULUS.

CHAPTER I.

LEAVING HOME.

WHEN a boy I loved to sing "From Afric's sunny fountains," and to read of Ledyard, Mungo Park, and other intrepid African explorers; but little did I then imagine that I should make the Dark Continent my home — be permitted to see the "king of beasts" walking about in his glory, the graceful antelope bounding from cliff to cliff, inhale the odor of its sweet flowers, bathe in its rivers, eat its luscious fruits, admire its scenery, and labor twoscore years for the evangelization of its inhabitants. But it has been even so.

What led me to select South Africa as my mission field may be briefly stated. While a member of the Theological Institute at East Windsor Hill, Conn., I belonged to a missionary society, the members of which agreed to examine carefully the claims of foreign missions, confer with each other, and ask the Lord to direct them as to their future fields of labor. Of our number, Benton went to Syria, Maynard to Salonica, and Rood, Wilder, and I to South Africa. The letters of Mr. Rood from the Zulu Mission, describing the language and character of the natives and urging the need of help, led me to conclude that I might be useful there, and on applying to the Prudential Committee of the American Board of Commissioners for Foreign Missions, I expressed a preference for that field. If I had received the reply, "You are needed elsewhere," I should have acquiesced. The hand of the Lord was upon me for good, and his guidance was clear in the selection of one who was to accompany me and share my solitude among the heathen. At my brother's parsonage, at Windham, Conn., I met a young lady whose home was in Northampton, Mass. If the consent of her parents could be obtained, she promised to go with me. Tremblingly, but hopefully, I went to ask. In considering the subject, they had decided to give their consent provided they liked the young man, and on condition that *he did not go to Africa.* After a pleasant interview and just as I was leaving, the mother inquired, "Mr. Tyler, to what part of the world do you propose going?" "To Africa," I replied. After a pause both said, "We have forgotten our conditions, but the Lord reigns. It is evidently his will that our daughter should go to Africa." Those good people never regretted the choice I had made of the Zulu Mission.

Some months intervened between graduation and the time of sailing, and instead of studying medicine, as I should have done, I supplied a pulpit in central Massachusetts and received a unanimous call to settle as pastor. Thank God, I did not waver in my determination to preach the gospel to the heathen! Rather suddenly the summons came from Boston, "Get ready at once; a ship is going to India which will stop at Cape Town." Hurrying to Northampton, I was married on the morning of February 27, 1849, to Miss Susan W. Clark. After the wedding breakfast, and singing

"Blest be the tie that binds,"

followed by a prayer, — only a part of which was heard, on account of sobs and sighs, too funeral-like altogether, — we started for East Windsor Hill, Conn., where I was to be ordained the next day.

Previous to the marriage I was asked to call on the family physician, who had known my intended wife from her childhood and was not at all pleased with the idea of her going to a heathen land. Rather abruptly Dr. T—— inquired: "Are you the young man who is going to take that delicate girl to Africa?" "Yes," I replied. "Well," said he, "mark my word: she will not live a year. Here is a box of medicines I present to you. Keep her alive as long as you can, but before the year is out I shall expect to hear of her death." Not very comforting, truly; but I consoled myself with the thought that not all physicians are infallible, and down in my heart of hearts I cherished the hope that I might some time in the future present that "delicate girl" to the doctor none the worse for her African experience. Twenty-three years later we revisited Northampton with our six children, all healthy, white Africans; but the doctor himself had passed away.

The ordination service was rather more solemn than is usual now on such occasions. It was difficult to make people believe that there was a single bright spot in Africa. The prevalent feeling was that we were going to our graves. What made the ordination, in my case, peculiarly pathetic was the fact that those who took part in it were near relatives. My brother-in-law preached the sermon, my father gave the charge, and my own brother the right hand of fellowship. Their addresses were published in a pamphlet form, and often, while engaged in mission work, I derived strength from their heartfelt utterances.

My own relatives, as well as those of my wife, placed no obstacles in the way of our going. The language of their hearts and lips was, "Go, and the Lord be with you." Some years after, my honored father remarked at a meeting of the American Board, of which he was a corporate member: "I have six children, and they all are a comfort to me; but none of them is so great a comfort as that son who is your missionary among the Zulus in South Africa. He is a beloved son and his wife is a beloved daughter; but if God will give them health to continue their labors I do not wish to see them again until I shall meet them in heaven."

Leaving Home.   21

Ordination over, we hurried to Boston to sail in the ship Concordia, bound to India by way of Cape of Good Hope. Our fellow-passengers, Rev. Hyman A. Wilder and Rev. Andrew Abraham, with their wives, were designated like ourselves to the Zulu Mission. We were fortunate in having a large ship, comfortable accommodations, and an agreeable captain. Vessels bound to South Africa in those days were scarce. They could hardly be found in sufficient numbers to take emigrants to the gold fields of California. The cargo to be landed at Cape Town consisted of flour and the first load of ice ever shipped to that port. The Dutch farmers residing there had not learned to appreciate such a luxury, and it proved an unprofitable speculation. Having received our instructions in due form in Park Street Church, we awaited the time of our departure, but lo! the cargo was not in the hold, the precise day could not be fixed, relatives could not wait to see us off, and we ourselves, becoming tired of Boston, revisited our homes, having to go through another edition of Baxter's Last Words. When we did sail at last, after a fervent prayer in the ship's cabin, there were two persons on whom our eyes were fixed, a dear brother and sister who lingered on the wharf to catch the last sight of those whom they never expected to see again in this world. Straining my eyes as long as possible, I was suddenly surprised by a rap on the shoulders, with an interrogatory from Wilder, my classmate and missionary brother: — "Tyler, are you not glad you are out of the dusty streets of Boston?" As Bunker Hill Monument grew smaller in the distance, we began to prepare for seasickness, and it was not long before we could each of us say as did Henry Ward Beecher, when he described that malady, " I felt — I felt — I felt — with a great deal of feeling." My wife was a terrible sufferer, growing weaker and weaker, until the captain alarmed me by saying, "If you don't do something for Mrs. Tyler, we shall have to bury her in the ocean." A powerful tonic set her right, and the voyage, though a long one, was on the whole pleasant.

At Cape Town we met with the kindest of friends. A letter of introduction from Dr. Carruthers, of Portland, Maine, to his old friend and brother Scotchman, Dr. Philip, superintendent of the London Missionary Society in South Africa, was a passport for Mrs. Tyler and myself, to a residence at the "mission house." Said Dr. Philip, "The bedroom you will occupy is that in which Dr. Vanderkemp, Robert Moffat, Livingstone, and other distinguished missionaries have slept." Though the doctor was aged and feeble, he had lost none of his Scottish wit and humor. He was a stanch Puritan, and sympathized heartily with the "old school" theology of New England.

Three weeks of delightful intercourse with the Christian people of Cape Town passed swiftly by, and then it was announced that the schooner Gem was ready to sail to Natal. In it we embarked, but alas, what a misnomer! A more untidy and uncomfortable craft I never saw. The voyage up the coast was long and stormy; the captain a drunkard, and incapable half of the time. I doubt whether gladder emotions sprang up in the heart of Vasco da Gama when he sighted Tierra Del Natalis on Christmas day than did in ours when we heard it said, "There is the bluff overhanging the harbor of Natal." Jubilant were we in the prospect of setting our feet on dry land, but our ardor was soon cooled by the words of the mate: "Don't be impatient; there is a bar to cross, and going over it is no joke." The sandbar, which choked the entrance of the harbor at that time, was truly formidable. There were only eight feet of water at high tide; the waves beat furiously over it, and accidents frequently occurred. Captain Homes, from America, crossing with his vessel a short time before our arrival, had the misfortune to see his own brother washed overboard, and before help could be rendered become the prey of a shark. We were told that the safest way for us was to go below and be shut up in the cabin, or we might share the same fate. Mr. Abraham and the ladies did so, but Mr. Wilder and myself chose to cling to the rigging. The Gem thumped several times on the bar, and was for a short time in danger of stranding, but no harm befell us, and in an hour we cast anchor in the most beautifully sheltered, land-locked harbor on the southeastern coast of Africa.

A boat immediately set off from the shore, and in it we were glad to see a gentleman who, we were told, was the Rev. Daniel Lindley. This pioneer missionary had sent to America a call for help, saying, "Come to our assistance. We will receive you as kindly as we know how. In us, if it be possible, you shall find the brothers and sisters you may leave behind." The warm welcome he gave us, "to the joys and toils of the African vineyard," made a deep impression on our hearts. I recall a rather brusque reply to a question I put to him, pointing to a party of Zulu men, semi-nude, and armed with clubs and spears, "Is it safe to dwell among this people?" "Brother Tyler," was the answer, "you are safer here than in the streets of Boston." It was difficult then to realize the truth of that observation, but subsequent experience proved that the good brother was right, and that life and property are more secure in a state of pure barbarism than in a state of godless civilization.

Our wives, I remember, were fearfully shocked by the sight of the savage-looking natives, and doubtless sympathized with the pioneer missionary ladies to the Sandwich Islands, who, when they saw the islanders for the first time, shut themselves up in their cabins, saying, "We cannot live among such people."

Durban, the seaport town of Natal, named after Sir Benjamin D'Urban, late governor at the Cape, was then a plain of sand. Only a few European families made their homes there, residing in wattle and daub houses; that is, dwellings made of twigs woven in and out of the posts and plastered with mud. No hotel existed, and but two or three stores, in which articles were sold at exorbitant prices. Just above the town was a large bush or jungle, called the "Berea" by Captain Allen Gardner, a philanthropic Englishman who once endeavored to establish a school there. When we first saw it, there were neither European nor Zulu dwellings; but elephants, lions, leopards, and other wild animals made it their habitat. G. C. Cato, Esq., American consul, banker, merchant, and general adviser, somewhat rough in speech and manner, but kindhearted and helpful, treated us most hospitably.

But we did not remain in Durban longer than was necessary to store our possessions in a warehouse, and were then ready for the wagon which came to take us to the mission station, located on a pretty river called Amanzimtote (Sweet Water). We were to take our first ride in a South African wagon, and I must describe that institution. It is a huge vehicle, on four immense wheels without springs, the body ten feet long, with a tent made of poles bent over, the ends of which are inserted in staples on the sides. Grass mats, painted canvas, and over all another piece of canvas unpainted, constitute the covering. This is tied to the sides of the wagon, and at night the ends are let down and fastened to the wheels. Inside is what is called in Natal, a *kartel*, simply a bed frame, made of four poles laced with strings of cow hide. On this is placed the mattress, for the wagon is the bedroom as well as the coach and parlor of the African missionary and traveler. Six or seven yoke of oxen, or a span, are considered necessary to draw this vehicle. Newcomers are disposed to pronounce it a cumbersome affair and behind the age; but they generally modify their opinion after a few months of travel over the rough roads of the country. The ox yoke is peculiar, being a pole about five feet long, three inches in diameter, and having four mortises to receive the keys, which take the place of bows in civilized countries. Each has a knob on the top to keep it from dropping through the mortise, and two notches on the outer edge, into one of which a strap is fastened, coming under the neck to keep the oxen in the yoke. This strap is made of buffalo hide with a loop at each end to fit it to the key. American farmers would laugh at this makeshift affair, but should they try it a while they would adopt it, if they had much to do with African bullocks.

Each wagon has a driver and "forelooper," or person to lead the oxen. The whip is of sea-cow's hide, the size of a man's finger, four or five yards long, to the end of which is

Traveling in South Africa.

attached a piece of buck's skin. The whipstock is the upper part of a bamboo cane, fifteen feet long. A dextrous driver soon impresses each ox in the span with a sense of its responsibility, besides making the "welkin ring" with a crack which on a still day is often mistaken in the distance for that of a rifle. A more exciting spectacle I have rarely seen than that of three spans united, forty-eight oxen in all, pulling a loaded wagon out of a bog, or up a steep hill, the drivers shouting and cracking their whips most furiously.

Mr. and Mrs. Wilder were to accompany us to Amanzimtote, on their way to the Ifumi station, and we prepared to take our first ride in Africa. "Start early," said Mr. Cato, "for you may have to ride in the dark." At six in the morning we said good-by to Durban, and launched out into what to us were unknown wilds. Neither the driver nor leader understood a word of English, and as we did not know Zulu we obtained no information from our sable attendants. After a *trek*, or journey of ten miles, we "outspanned," that is, unyoked, the oxen, to let them feed, and also to refresh ourselves. In the wagon chest we found all that was requisite: a kettle, matches, dishes, knives, forks, bread, butter, tea, coffee, sugar, etc. Mrs. Adams knew what we needed and had kindly provided for us. This was the first picnic we enjoyed in South Africa, an antepast of many similar ones in the future. At three P.M. we started, but were soon obliged to halt. The oxen, unable to pull the heavy wagon up a sandy hill, were turned out to graze. The sun beginning to sink behind the horizon, I remember debating with brother Wilder as to which one of us should keep watch at night, with a loaded rifle, to defend the party from wild beasts. Our hearts were soon gladdened by the unexpected arrival of a new span of fresh and strong bullocks, sent by Dr. Adams to our relief. A new driver also came, who could speak a little English. "Are you the new missionaries? How do you like our country?" etc. The wagon was set in motion and at nine o'clock a light was pointed out to us as that of Dr. Adams' house. The welcome we received more than paid us for all our fatigue.

CHAPTER II.

STUDY OF THE LANGUAGE.

AN own brother and sister could not have made our stay at Amanzimtote more pleasant than did Dr. Adams and his wife. Unremitting in their kindness to us in all things, they helped us especially to get a good start in the acquisition of the Zulu dialect. They were model missionaries. Of the pioneer band which left America in 1834, they had clung to the Zulu field in the midst of great discouragements. More indefatigable laborers in the mission field I have never known. They wrote but little for The Missionary Herald, and on that account Christians in this country knew little of them and their work. The doctor's knowledge of medicine and uniform readiness to help the bodies of the natives won for him easy access to their hearts. He gained their confidence and affection. From a distance of forty or fifty miles they came to him for consultation and help. Improving every opportunity to sow the good seed, he saw that they carried it with them to their homes, and in after years the fruits appeared. That the natives trusted him to a remarkable degree is evident from the fact that on one occasion, when they were inclined to rebel against the English government, their chiefs were sent to talk with the doctor and obtain his advice before taking up arms. Listening patiently to all their complaints, he questioned them as to what would be the result of the rebellion; suggested the loss of life and property that would follow, and opened their eyes to some aspects of the case which they had not considered. Putting their hands to their mouths in Zulu fashion, when new light breaks in upon their minds, they acknowledged the wisdom of their teacher and went home resolved to keep quiet. I am glad to say that Sir Theophilus Shepstone, secretary for native affairs in Natal, took notice of this act, and thanked Dr. Adams most heartily for saving the colony from war.

Dr. Adams labored eleven years before he saw any fruit. The first individual to come out of heathenism — indeed the first Zulu convert — was Umbulazi, a woman who had fled from her kraal to the mission station in a state of starvation. She often said to Mrs. Adams, "God raised me from the dust of the earth. When I first came to you, I was eating herbs and grass, because I could get nothing else. I cared for nobody and nobody cared for me; but the Lord told me to go to the missionary and he would help me."

The image of that mother rises before me. A poor woman, depressed by cruel treatment and disowned by her nearest friends, had heard this missionary preach the gospel of love, and thinking that the bearer of such a message must be merciful to her, an outcast, threw herself down at his door, where he found her, with her little son on her back, waiting for admittance. Her whole appearance and manners were repulsive, but the longing for sympathy and love which her words indicated was fully met by those faithful workers for Christ. They had prayed and labored that even *one* soul might be given them, and what joy they must have felt when after much instruction the light of the gospel seemed to dawn on her dark mind. Then she stood forth alone, a professed believer in that new faith, which was her comfort and support for nearly thirty years, until death reunited her to those sainted ones who had guided her to heaven. The last time I saw her in her feebleness and blindness, she took my hand and said, "I am ready to go home to my father and mother," meaning the missionary and his wife. "The Lord has been good to me. He has permitted me to see great things." Is it not interesting to remember that the light of the gospel first shone in a *woman's* heart among the Zulus?

The next convert was a woman with whom Umbulazi was accustomed to pray in a cluster of bushes near the station. Still another woman, who was trying to become a witch doctress, came to the station, and was soon "clothed and in her right mind." Mrs. Adams remarked in regard to her, "The last time I saw that woman, I said to myself. 'You are a hopeless case, surely.'" At the time of our visit at Amanzimtote, there was considerable religious interest, and the hearts of those faithful workers were greatly encouraged. At a communion season which we attended seven persons were received into church fellowship. The sermon that day was on the text, "Fear not, little flock," etc. As it was in Zulu I could not understand it; but the deep attention given, and tears that occasionally trickled down the cheeks of the auditors, showed that it made a deep impression.

Dr. Adams died in 1851, of overwork, at the age of forty-five, and was buried at the station which now bears his name. Mrs. Adams remained in the field five years after the death of her husband, and then, on account of failing health, returned to this country. She always looked back on her life in Africa with joy, and on the morning of her last day on earth spoke of her love for the missionary band there and for the Zulu people. She died in Cleveland, Ohio. Both Dr. and Mrs. Adams laid a broad and deep foundation for the future. Who can doubt that their reward in heaven is great?

We should have been glad to remain with those good missionaries a year at least, to become imbued with their spirit, and so accustomed to their *modus operandi* in mission work that we could reflect it in after life. But the custom in those days was to send newcomers, as soon as possible, to their stations, so we

Study of the Language. 33

addressed ourselves, with all our might, to the mastery of the language. No grammar or dictionary had been published. Only a few words had been collected to aid in the formation of sentences. The regularity and flexibility of the dialect struck us at first with surprise and pleasure, and the more we studied it, the more we admired it. It is, like the Italian, abounding in vowels, and is both pleasing to the ear and easy to speak. There is great poverty of words expressing moral thoughts, but this is not surprising when we consider the absence of such thoughts in the native mind.

Mr. Grout doubts "if the German, Greek, or any other language can exceed the Zulu in the scope and liberty it gives for the formation of derivative words."

The names of persons in Zulu are derived from circumstances connected with their birth. For instance, if a small snake happens to be seen or killed when a boy is born he is called Unyokana, " a little snake.' If honey is plentiful at such a time, the child is named Unyosi, the name of that luxury. Should the infant be a large one he receives the appellation Ungagumuntu, "as large as a man." If there happens to be a fire at his birth, the babe is named Unomlilo, "with fire."

The time required to learn the language so as to be understood by the natives depends on the facility one has for the acquisition of foreign tongues. Missionaries in Natal have been known to preach in Zulu six months after their arrival. A year or more is required before one can catch what the natives say, they speak so rapidly. Zulus are remarkably patient, and do not laugh at mistakes made by young missionaries unless they are calculated to provoke their risibilities beyond control. One who, perhaps, began to preach too early had confounded the word *lalani*, meaning "go to sleep," with *lalelani*, signifying "give attention." He began his sermon one Sunday with the former, "*Lalani, nonke* (Go to sleep, all of you)." Another missionary, in giving directions to a native lad in reference to knocking to pieces some hard sods in the field, used the word for wizards, *abatagati* instead of *amayabati* (sods), saying, "*Hamba u tyaye abatagati* (Go and knock the wizards in pieces)." The boy thought a difficult task was assigned him. The wife of a missionary, wishing to have a young man kill two ducks, had not noticed that the word for men differed from that for ducks in one letter: *Amadoda* (men), *amadada* (ducks). She said to him, "*Hamba bulala amadoda amabili* (Go and kill two men)." The young man looking up with a smile asked, "Which men shall I kill?"

Rev. Daniel Lindley.

CHAPTER III.

OUR MISSION STATION.

I HAVE described the ox-wagon, a large affair, but none too large for the missionary's needs. Nor are the oxen required to draw it (twelve or fourteen in number) too many for the rough roads, steep hills, and sandy beds of the rivers. In addition to furniture, dishes, food, and clothing, it was necessary to take tools for house building. I was fortunate in having for a companion and adviser the good brother who gave us such a warm reception when we landed. Mr. Lindley had said, "I will see you settled in your new home;" and his experience and tact were of incalculable help. Esidumbini lay fifty miles north of Durban, and that was my nearest market and post office. We were three days on the journey, but the trip was enlivened by the narrative Mr. Lindley gave of incidents connected with his early life and African experiences, which I will briefly record. When the American Board of Commissioners for Foreign Missions decided to establish a mission in South Africa, among the six heroic young men who responded to the call was the son of Rev. Jacob Lindley, D.D., an eminent Presbyterian minister. That son was Daniel, and at the time he was pastor of a church in North Carolina. His people, some of them slaveholders, were ardently attached to him, and when they received the tidings that he had decided to go to Africa, it is hard to say which predominated, astonishment or indignation. I asked him how he succeeded in getting away. He replied, "I preached four sermons on the kingdom of God, and one on the Great Commission, and if ever I preached from my heart I did then. My people saw that the call was from God, and gave me up, saying, 'It is His will that you should go.'"

It is to be regretted that no careful history has been published of Mr. Lindley's labors, trials, narrow escapes, disappointments at first, but afterwards encouragements. Had he committed to paper his experiences, as he occasionally gave them in public and private, they would have been quite as interesting and romantic as those of Rev. Robert Moffat.

Of this lamented brother, considered as a preacher or platform speaker, I am not in danger of speaking too highly. Many in the United States who heard him have said that no foreign missionary surpassed him. Owing to a keen knowledge of human nature, he seemed to know just what to say to interest an audience, and was always adequate to the occasion. As a hint of the kind of missionary addresses best adapted to interest and edify public audiences, he related an incident which came under his own observation. Seated in the vestry of a church in Connecticut, previous to entering the pulpit, the pastor asked him upon what he was about to speak. Mr. Lindley replied that he always aimed in his missionary addresses to tell the audience about the people among whom he labored, their customs, worship, etc., and the nature of his work among them. Said Dr. ——: "I am glad to hear you say this, for a few months ago we had here a missionary from India who occupied a full hour in trying to show my people how they might save money for the heathen. One of my deacons, a shrewd merchant, came to me and said: 'We Yankees do not need to be told how to save money, but how to use it.'"

When it was decided that Mr. Lindley return to America to spend the evening of his days, there was great mourning on the part of his friends, black and white. At the farewell meeting, one of the native preachers, in a most pathetic address, said: "We have met to bury our father and mother. Our missionary knows all, from the governor to the poorest man, and he is called by all 'father.' His wife has taught our wives, and by precept upon precept and an unwavering example of goodness and faithfulness, has done her work for Christ." A collection was then taken up of one hundred dollars, which was sent to America, to be held in trust to "bury their father and mother, when they should die." A clergyman in New York City spoke truly when he said, "Such demonstrations from such a source are infinitely more honorable to humanity and America, as nobly represented by her missionary, than all the victories that British soldiers have won in Asia or Africa since Warren Hastings became master of India."

Our ride to Esidumbini in an ox-wagon was to me, a newcomer, full of interest. Occasionally a large *inhlangu* (reed buck) of a gray, ashy color, with its beautiful horns measuring fifteen inches or more from tip to tip, would jump out of the long grass, run a distance of fifty yards, then stop, turn around and look at us. Mr. Lindley was not slow to seize his rifle, and the poor buck paid the penalty of having gazed too long at the disturbers of his quiet. So numerous were antelopes of various kinds and sizes, that there was no necessity to go out of our way for them. Stopping at a Dutchman's farm the last day of our ride, he surprised me by giving away all the venison we had in the wagon. When I asked him what we should eat, he replied, "I will shoot another buck to-morrow morning." He was as good as his word. About sunrise, as I was boiling the kettle for our coffee, I heard the report of a rifle, and then a voice saying, "Send the natives for a buck I have killed." It was a fine animal, weighing about one hundred pounds.

On a beautiful afternoon we came in sight of my future home. The air was clear, and, as we reached the end of a long table-land, a deep and wide valley, filled with undulating hills and winding streams with an occasional waterfall, suddenly opened on our view. On one side was a dense thicket sloping toward a river six miles distant, where elephants, lions, buffaloes, leopards, hyenas, and other wild beasts held undisputed sway. In the *kloofs*, or ravines, were trees of considerable size, but the hills abounded with the low, prickly mimosa, amid which we discerned clusters of native huts.

How to descend into this valley from the table-land, with no wagon path, was a puzzling question. Ledges of rock occasioned great risk of upsetting the wagon. As a native boy led the oxen by the strap attached to their horns, we helped to keep them from going too fast by throwing stones at their heads shouting, " Ah, now! Ah, now!" and as the sun was sinking behind the horizon we outspanned by the side of a beautiful stream.

Before making preparations for supper, Mr. Lindley said to me, " Brother Tyler, this valley is to be your home. Let us take possession of it in the name of King Immanuel." We knelt on the ground by the side of the wagon, and a prayer ascended to heaven from the lips of that good missionary which I shall never forget. It was that his young, inexperienced brother might at all times " have an untiring patience and an unwavering faith," qualities which I found essential in my subsequent career. After a day or two of advice and assistance, Mr. Lindley returned home, and I was thrown upon my own resources.

It is impossible to write of Mr. Lindley, and not mention his wife, one of the most devoted missionary ladies who ever set foot on African soil. Belonging to the pioneer band, Mrs. Lindley suffered great privations and hardships, but throughout all she labored incessantly and always cheerfully and with bright hopes for the future. Notwithstanding her large family and the cares which devolved upon her, she found time to teach the natives as well as her own children.

She would be most accurately represented with a baby on her lap, pointing out the letters to a Zulu kneeling beside her, or explaining to a company of native women a portion of the Bible.

Her labors were not in vain. A number of native preachers, two of whom were ordained, received their first religious impressions from her earnest appeals. She died in New York City, November 22, 1877. Mr. Lindley died in Morristown, N. J., September 22, 1888, at the age of eighty.

At the funeral service at the Fourth Avenue Presbyterian Church in New York, the following remark was made: "The world stoops to honor the memories and achievements of men who have won great successes in war, politics, and business by merely selfish methods and for selfish objects. Some day or other it will place, far above all these heroes of an hour, the men who have emulated the spirit and equaled the achievements of the founders of the Christian Church."

A ZULU KRAAL.

CHAPTER IV.

LIFE IN A KRAAL.

THE place for building selected, and the trees cut and brought out of the kloofs on native shoulders, I found it necessary to use the wagon in hauling the timber, so my bedroom and parlor had to be given up. My wife was at a mission station twenty miles away. Where should I lodge? In a kraal surely, if I could obtain permission of its owner.

A kraal throughout South Africa is simply a collection of huts arranged about a circular fence of thorns which encloses the cattle fold. This fence is eight or ten feet high, with a stronger and larger one outside the huts, walling in the whole. The number of huts corresponds to the number of wives belonging to the owner or headman. There are, however, in various parts of South Africa, military kraals with two hundred huts or more, in which are quartered the king's soldiers, young and middle-aged men, ready to enter the field at a moment's call. The huts are made of long wattles or poles, the ends of which are fastened in the ground, the tops being bent over and lashed together with the "monkey rope," a vine well suited for the purpose. A strong basket-like roof is thus constructed, which is supported by horizontal poles resting on two or more upright posts. The covering, of long grass, is kept from being blown away by small rods sharpened at each end, bent bow-like, and fastened to the network underneath. On the top of the hut skulls and horns of oxen are frequently placed, probably designed as ornaments. To a newcomer approaching a kraal, the huts bear a striking resemblance to large haycocks. They are impervious to rain, and are made so strong that no wild animal, except an elephant, has been known to destroy them. Their location is ordinarily on a hillside, to prevent the rain from settling near them or entering the pits in the cattle fold in which their grain is kept. Indian corn, with other cereals, and beans are thus stored away from the weevils and white ants. These pits are about six feet deep and as large as a hogshead, but shaped more like a jar, with a covering of flat stones and earth. The entrance to a Zulu hut is about two feet high in the middle and three feet wide at the base. The inhabitants go in and out on their hands and knees. The door is of pliant sticks woven together and made to correspond in size to the opening. In royal kraals there is generally one hut surpassing all others in the beauty and skill with which it is constructed. The principal pole or wattle spanning the entire arch is called "*intingo jenkosikazi* (the wattle of the queen)." The rainbow has the same designation.

Life in a Kraal.   43

The interior of a well-kept Zulu habitation is not so repulsive as one might suppose who has never inspected it. First, the floor presents the appearance of polished ebony, having been made of a glutinous kind of earth which has passed through the mouths of innumerable white ants. This is pounded hard, rubbed with smooth stones, and then smeared with fresh cow dung. Some Zulu women take pride in having their floors shine so that you can almost see your face reflected in them as in a mirror. The fireplace is a saucer-like excavation in the center of the floor, with a rim around it six inches high to keep the firebrands and ashes from scattering. Around this the inhabitants sit or lounge, chatting, singing, scolding, snuffing, smoking, or dozing. At night grass mats are spread over the floor, on which they sleep with their feet towards the fire in cold weather. Their pillows are small wooden stools, about five inches high, on which they rest their necks, not their heads. To foreigners this not only appears uncomfortable, but too suggestive of a guillotine to be agreeable; but the Zulus are too proud of their elaborate headdress to bring it into contact with the ground.

Calabashes for sour milk, earthen pots (homemade) for water or beer, or for cooking purposes, constitute the chief utensils of a Zulu pantry.

The natives are very fond of meat of various kinds: beef, mutton, venison. Pork is also eaten; and lard for anointing their bodies is a great luxury. They dislike eggs and have an abhorrence for fish. They cultivate Indian corn, pumpkins, *amadumbi*, a species of caladium, the root of which is eaten; and, since introduced by the whites, beans and sweet potatoes are favorite vegetables. Indian corn is their staple breadstuff, but it is usually eaten boiled like mush. Stewed pumpkin is also mixed with Indian meal. Thickened sour milk is to them a luxury. Missionaries and other foreigners, after they have become accustomed to it, also greatly like it. In hot weather it is the nearest approach to ice cream of anything obtainable in Africa. New milk is turned into a calabash and left to sour, fresh milk being added daily, and when it is properly soured a plug at the bottom of the calabash is removed, the whey escapes, and the milk is poured into an earthen dish. It is about the consistency of "bonny-clabber." Boiled corn, ground on stones and mixed with sour milk, is food of which the Zulus never tire.

Another article of food, or drink rather, is beer brewed from musty Indian corn. Well-to-do natives make this in large quantities, hence it is not unusual to see in a hut a huge earthen pot that will hold twenty or thirty gallons. The mill for grinding corn and other articles is a large stone, two or three feet in length, in which an indentation has been made, together with a small one, oval-shaped and double the size of a man's fist. The material ground, or mashed, falls upon a small grass

A ZULU HUT.

mat placed by the side of the stone. Every hut has in it one of these primitive but useful mills.

At night other occupants than human beings find lodging in a Zulu house. These are goats and calves, tied to a stake in a small enclosure fenced off for their accommodation, besides, occasionally, rats and cockroaches too numerous to mention.

In one of these huts I spent the first six weeks of my missionary life. The kraal numbered six dwellings, and the owner, for a reasonable compensation, placed the best one at my disposal. A screen of blankets hid me from the eyes of my sable companions when the time came for retiring. I was careful to see that the entrance was closed at night to keep out all members of the serpent family. Not fancying the process of creeping in and out on all fours day after day, I requested of the proprietor of the harem the privilege of inserting an upright door of civilized construction, telling him that when I left I would leave it for his accommodation. His reply was, " My fathers went in on their hands and knees, and I shall continue to do so, and, moreover, while you are among the Zulus you must do as the Zulus do."

An appeal to ancestral custom was the argument the natives invariably used to rebut all reasons why they should abandon their absurd practices as well as their superstitious worship. Pointing one day to the cattle fold in which

manure lay four or five feet deep, and also a
huge pile of ashes outside the kraal, I asked:
"Why don't you use these valuable ferti-
lizers?" The only answer I received was: "It
is not our custom."[1]

In the hut the smoke, having no chimney
through which to escape, was my greatest
annoyance. At the end of six weeks I did
not regret exchanging this smoky abode for a
larger one, with the improvements of a door
and window, and a partition dividing the bedroom from the sitting room. A kitchen was
built outside, in which was placed an American stove. Then I thought it time to send for
my wife, and on her arrival everything assumed
a changed appearance. I have always been
glad that I had this opportunity of living for
a time in immediate contact with the natives.
I caught their intonations and mastered the
"clicks" of the language. At times it was
difficult to repress feelings of disgust at the
sight of unblushing impurity, and the sound
of dancing, yelling, grumbling, and quarreling,
but a voice within me said: "The incarnate
and spotless Saviour saw what was far more
revolting to him than anything I behold;" and
I found the people possessed some interesting
traits of character despite their environment.
The Zulus, like other African tribes, are naturally proud, independent, and suspicious of
the white man's curiosity; but there is a way

---

[1] I afterward ascertained that superstitious fears had something
to do with this.

to unlock the door of their hearts. Occasionally creeping into one of their huts, and watching the careworn housewife busy at her daily tasks, I dropped a kind word which generally met with a smile or some token of appreciation. Nothing pleased the parents more than my attempts to amuse the children, as they rolled about on the floor, innocent of clothing, their eyes sparkling with humor, and their teeth shining like polished ivory. When I could assist them in secular matters I did so. By attending to their bodily wants I was enabled to reach their hearts. I had daily evidence of the wisdom of the remark of St. Francis Xavier: "The smallest acts of friendship, an obliging word and civil look, are no despicable part of the missionary's armor." The confidence of the people was won. They looked upon me as their friend, although they were wedded to their superstitions. At first compassion was awakened in view of their degradation, then love, and a longing for their salvation. Love begat love. When Mrs. Tyler became acquainted with them she experienced the same emotions. It was not long before the natives said, "See how she loves us!"

CHAPTER V.

HOUSE BUILDING.

THE site for my house was on a hill commanding a fine view of the mountains in Zululand to the north, an immense plateau or table-land to the west, and to the east the Indian Ocean, visible through a ravine, the bed of the Umhlali River. The scenery was so varied and picturesque we never tired of it. The atmosphere was exceedingly clear and exhilarating. Esidumbini seemed a perfect sanitarium, and we rejoiced in having found so healthy and beautiful a place of residence.

But as to the building of a house, we did not fancy living longer than was necessary in a hut with so few accommodations. In my boyhood I had often seen house builders at work, but never took notes with a view to doing anything of the kind in after life. However, I knew enough to use the line, lay out the ground, see that holes were dug at proper distances for posts, and that they were firmly erected, after their lower ends were charred to prevent their being eaten immediately by white ants, and also that the beams were pinned to the posts; but how to make rafters I knew not. I wrote my dilemma to a good brother missionary, Rev. Aldin Grout, living twenty-five miles distant, and he came at once to my aid. Reaching us at three P.M., he rested a while, and then went out to inspect my operations. I can still see the smile on his countenance as he beheld my long face and heard me dilate on my troubles. Throwing off his coat, workman fashion, he began to show me in a thoroughly practical manner what was to be done. Selecting a few poles he told me to take them to a certain spot, drive down a peg, arrange a couple in the form of a triangle, bore the holes, pin the poles together, and saw off the ends properly, making me do the work that I might not forget in future. In less than two hours all the rafters were put together, and before Mr. Grout left the next morning a good part of the roof was up. Easy enough, I thought, if you only know how.

Mr. Grout was one of the pioneer missionaries who sailed from Boston in 1834.[1] He

[1] A gentleman, now nearly eighty years old, who was residing in Cape Town at the time the six pioneer missionaries of the American Board of Commissioners for Foreign Missions landed there, thus speaks of a meeting in connection with the Sabbath-school, held in the Union Chapel: —

"A man who had something to do in making arrangements for the meeting had placed on the communion table a plate of biscuits and a decanter of wine. One of the missionaries, being called on to address the meeting, gave such a speech that he astonished us all. He began by expressing his amazement at finding one present who was the instigator to all evil. He detailed the crimes of which men are guilty, and attributed them all to this one who was in our midst. Then he turned upon us present for allowing such an one to enter the house of God, that no one had raised his voice, or prevented his entrance, and when he had excited us to the utmost by his condemnation of this miscreant, he pointed to the wine."

That missionary was Rev. Aldin Grout, now living in Springfield, Mass., at the advanced age of nearly ninety.

Soon after the above incident, Mr. Grout, with some clergymen landed in Natal early in 1835, with Dr. Adams and Rev. George Champion. Hopefully and zealously Mr. Grout began missionary work in Zululand, then under Dingaan, a cruel despot. The difficulties under which he labored and the perils by which he was surrounded were sufficient to intimidate the most courageous.

He attempted to teach Dingaan to read. The proud king said to Mr. Grout, "Why have you come to me?"

"To teach and preach the gospel to you," Mr. Grout replied.

Said his sable majesty, "Do you then presume to think that you can teach me anything that I do not already know?"

It was explained to him that he must first learn the letters of the alphabet.

"Can I now learn to read?" he inquired.

Mr. Grout told him that he would come again on the morrow and give him a lesson.

"But can so great a thing be put off till to-morrow? Let me have them all now," responded the chief.

Mr. Grout then printed the whole twenty-four letters, and began, as he said, "to educate a king in a day."

Soon, on repeating the letters he had learned,

---

in Cape Town, was invited to dine at the house of Rev. Dr. Philip, superintendent of the London Missionary Society in South Africa, and the good doctor, seeing the missionary's eyes directed to the decanter of wine in its usual place on the table, called his servant to remove it, and that was the last time it was placed on that table. It required some degree of moral courage in those days to set one's "face like a flint" against the drinking usages of society, and I love to recall what the missionary, then a young man, so heroically did.

the king was at a loss, and said, "I have forgotten that one."

"Well, it is D."

Soon the king had forgotten another, and another, and became confused and forgot all. In his vexation he threw down the paper, saying, "There, I told you I could not learn. No, I do not want you; you may go home."

On another occasion, while Mr. Grout was showing Dingaan his medicines, a small pair of tweezers was observed, and the king asked, "What is that for?" Mr. Grout replied, "To extract splinters or small ticks from the body." The response came, "I will take that for my own use." Soon after he appropriated a bottle of smelling salts, and Mr. Grout began to think that he had better keep his things out of sight if he wished to preserve them.

Asking one day for medicine, as he had a severe cold on his chest, a mustard poultice was recommended. The king had it applied first to one of his people that he might watch its effects before he tried it himself.

Mr. Grout's love for the Zulu Mission was tested in the early days of its history. On account of war between the Zulus and Dutch farmers and the discouraging prospects, the American Board recalled Mr. Grout and his colaborers, Lindley and Adams; but before the summons from Boston reached them, the darkest days had passed. They could not brook the idea of retreating from the field. Their hearts were buoyed up with a faith kindred to that which inspired the "apostle to the Karens," eighteen years previously, who, when asked, "What prospect of ultimate success is there?" replied, "As much as that there is an almighty and faithful God."

Dr. Adams said, "I will support myself by my profession." Mr. Lindley, no less courageous, observed, "And I will obtain a living by teaching the children of the Dutch Boers." Mr. Grout declared that he would "go home and plead for the continuance of the mission." To quote his own words: "With hearts well-nigh broken, myself and wife took passage, and in 1844 were safely landed in Cape Town. For nearly ten years we had been in search of a place where we could stop long enough to preach the gospel and witness its fruits, and now, without any intimation that we had done any material good, we were called away. We had hardly landed in Cape Town before friends began to inquire, 'Why have you left your work? You must go back. If funds are all you want, they shall be forthcoming.'"

Sir Peregrine Maitland, then governor at the Cape, gave Mr. Grout an appointment as government missionary, saying, "It is a pity men should leave a place and people just as they have learned enough of the language to enable them to be useful," and adding, "I think more of missionaries than of soldiers to keep savages quiet."

A purse of £170 was contributed by the good people of Cape Town for immediate necessities, and in June, 1844, Mr. Grout returned to Natal.

He was remarkably adapted to mission work in South Africa, and his efforts were attended with success, though he labored more than ten years before seeing his first convert. Failing health rendered it necessary that he should come to America to spend the evening of his days, but he has often regretted that he did not conclude to remain in Africa and die among his own people. When he left this country in 1834 he was accused by some of "going on a wild-goose chase;" but he used to say, "I have caught my goose."

His first wife died in the early history of the mission, leaving one daughter, Mrs. Ireland, now in the Natal field. With his second wife he has lately celebrated his golden wedding. May his last days be radiant with the divine presence!

I must say that my new house, when completed and occupied, seemed to me like a palace. The months flew by rapidly and pleasantly, each finding us better able to communicate with the people. We had Indian corn, amadumbi, and occasionally meat brought to us for sale by the natives. Fowls we could obtain cheaply, and in abundance. With my rifle I frequently shot antelopes that were quietly feeding near by.

One privation, keenly felt during the first few years, was the absence of news, except at long intervals. The nearest post office was fifty miles distant, and, native young men being needed for work of various kinds, weeks sometimes passed before we could send one for our letters. Natal could not then boast of a newspaper. Tidings reached us one day that filled our hearts with joy. An American vessel had arrived, bringing not only a mail from home, but other things "too numerous to mention," as our Durban agent wrote. Immediately were dispatched two able-bodied Zulus, with the promise that if they would return before bedtime the following Saturday (it was then Wednesday) each would receive a shilling extra. They took two large bags, each holding as much as a flour barrel, in which to bring the newly-arrived articles. Saturday night came; it was dark and rainy, and the prospect of seeing our carriers grew fainter and fainter. Ten o'clock came, and just as we concluded to retire a rap was heard on our door. There were the two Zulu men with immense burdens on their heads, their bodies covered with perspiration. To terrify wild animals and ward off witches, they said they had sung and shouted all the way after sundown. The huge bags were placed on the dining room floor; something tempting to the appetites of the messengers given them, and we began to inspect this first arrival of things from the dear ones at home.

Opening the bags I poured out their contents. The Eclectic, Harper's Monthly, The Missionary Herald, and other publications were laid one side; boxes of maple sugar, little bags of walnuts and butternuts, parcels of clothing, an album, bedquilt, daguerreotypes, etc., gladdened our eyes and hearts. Then we sat down to read some of the welcome letters out of a big bundle before us. When twelve o'clock came we laid all aside to be reinspected on Monday morning.

Mrs. Tyler, writing about that time to a friend in this country, observed, " You ask if we never 'cast one longing, lingering look behind,' and if it does not make us sad to think of you all. Perhaps you will hardly think me sincere if I tell you 'No.' I don't know that I have ever felt, since the time I stepped from the plank which connected our ship with land, that I have had a desire to live in America. I do not mean that I love my native land any the less, or that I should not love to visit it again; but I would rather live at Esidumbini and labor for the good of the many souls that are famishing for the lack of knowledge, and here too would I die. I feel that it is my home and I love it. I love my friends so dearly that it seems unnatural not to see them occasionally; but I knew it would be hard before I came here, and tried to make up my mind to leave them all at home and be content to write to them, and hope to receive many letters from them. The more I become acquainted and interested in our people, the more I shall learn to give up all other objects of thought which would tend to make me unhappy."

Then referring to her husband, she said: "We try to help each other in all sorts of ways. When Mr. Tyler is putting on a door-latch, and turns it upside down and wonders why it does not work, I run and help him; and when I make similar mistakes, or need a little bookshelf or something of that sort, he is always ready to help me. So we conclude, like other young married people, that we were made for each other."

A HEATHEN ZULU YOUNG MAN.

CHAPTER VI.

ZULU DRESS.

THE clothing of the Zulus in their normal state is too scanty to require much description. Mark Twain's observation in regard to the Sandwich Islanders is not inapplicable to this people: "They wear — they wear — they wear a smile, and some of them a hat and a pair of spectacles." The dress worn by the men consists of a girdle of ox hide from which is suspended in front a bunch of the tails of monkeys, wild cats, or other animals, and at the back a small apron of ox hide or the skin of some wild beast.

The garment of a woman is a skirt of pliable tanned leather, lubricated with fat. The bridal skirt is trimmed with beads of divers colors and a rich profusion of brass buttons. This is a present from the bridegroom, with which the young damsel is as much pleased as are her civilized sisters in other lands with their jewels, laces, and orange blossoms. Belts and semi-belts are worn by young men and women, the more beads ornamenting them the better.

Zulu men are dressmakers as well as tailors, making all the garments of the women as well as their own.

Washing day is not one to be dreaded among

this people. Should a garment require cleansing, it is taken to the river and rubbed with the fibrous root of an alkaline plant which takes the place of soap.

The native headdress occupies considerable attention. Married men shave all the upper part of the head except the crown, on which they leave a little wool in a circular shape about four inches in diameter. To this is sewn a gutta-percha-like ring, made of gum and charcoal. With the growth of the wool the ring rises sometimes to the height of six inches. Into this ring they thrust long snuff spoons, porcupine quills, needles, and other articles of utility. This ring is a badge of manhood and respectability. Violence done to it is quickly and bitterly resented. Men have chosen to die rather than be deprived of it. Under the old Zulu kings no man was allowed to wear the ring till he had distinguished himself in battle.

While Rev. Robert Moffat was on a visit to Mosilekatzi, king of the Matabele Zulus, a man was brought before the chief to receive his sentence for a crime, the penalty of which was death. Mr. Moffat earnestly interceded for his life. The story from the missionary's own pen is too interesting to be omitted: —

"'The prisoner, though on his knees, had something dignified in his mien. Not a muscle of his countenance moved, but a bright black eye indicated a feeling of intense interest, which the swerving balance between life and death only could produce. The case required little investigation; the charges were clearly substantiated, and the culprit pleaded guilty. But, alas! he knew that it was at a bar where none ever heard the heart-reviving sound of pardon, even for offenses small compared with his!

"A pause ensued, during which the silence of death pervaded the assembly. At length the monarch spoke, and, addressing the prisoner, said: 'You are a dead man; but I shall do to-day what I never did before. I spare your life for the sake of my friend and father. I know that his heart weeps at the shedding of blood; for his sake I spare your life; but you must be degraded for life; you must no more associate with the nobles of the land, nor enter the towns of the princes of the people, nor even again mingle in the dance of the mighty. Go to the poor of the field and let your companions be the inhabitants of the desert.'

"The sentence passed, the hardened man was expected to bow in grateful admiration. But, no! Holding his hand clasped on his bosom, he replied: 'O king, afflict not my heart! I have incited thy displeasure. Let me be slain like the warrior. I cannot live with the poor.' Raising his hand to the ring he wore on his head, he continued: 'How can I live among the dogs of the king, and disgrace this badge of honor which I have won among the spears and shields of the mighty? Let me die, O Pe Zulu!'"

"His request was granted, and his hands were tied erect over his head. Now my exertions to save his life were vain. He disdained the boon on the conditions offered, preferring to die with the honors he had won at the point of the spear. He was led forth, a man walking on each side. My eyes followed him until he reached the top of a high precipice, over which he was precipitated into the deep part of the river beneath, where the crocodiles, accustomed to such meals, were yawning to devour him ere he could reach the bottom."

Shaving the head is not confined to Zulu men. Married women do the same, leaving, however, a topknot for which they have a great regard. A mixture of red ochre and grease makes this topknot an agreeable ornament in their estimation. A few of them, however, do not shave at all, but rub their wool with red pigment, making it look more like a mop than anything else. Witch doctresses fasten to such a headdress the bladders of birds or of wildcats, blown out, and thus appear hideous in the extreme.

Young men not married allow their hair to grow, dressing it in a variety of fantastic shapes. Now it looks like a sugar loaf, now like two little hills with valleys between. The more rancid butter, or mutton tallow, or cocoanut oil they can get to rub on their heads the better. Odoriferous substances are freely used, especially before going into company, and perfumes are now bought largely from English merchants. Places of worship need ample ventilation, particularly when filled with Zulus freshly lubricated. Missionaries not only require grace, but strong olfactory nerves, and they often sigh for a different kind of anointing.

Zulus of both sexes and of all ages are exceedingly fond of ornaments. Necklaces, made of beads of various colors, are common. Brass rings, some of them we should think too cumbersome to be agreeable, are worn on the arms and legs. The head is decked with feathers, from those of the common fowl to the ostrich and the most beautiful birds of the forest. A young man is sometimes seen with a pair of deer's horns attached to his forehead, while about his neck are strung leopard's teeth, pieces of crocodile skin, bits of wood, claws of birds, and small bags of medicine. "Spirit" or "witch" doctors commonly wear long leopard skins dangling about their feet. Infants have holes bored in their ears which are enlarged as they grow older, and made the receptacle for ivory knobs or reed snuffboxes. Flowers are often seen on the head, one of which, the "love-making posy," is said to foster the tender passion. Young men generally wear this when paying attention to the ladies. On the arms and bosoms of women raised scars are often noticeable. These were made in infancy, and in the gashes cut in the skin were inserted charcoal and ashes from the bones of serpents. The operation must be painful, but when ornamentation is considered, bodily suffering is not regarded. An ornament of which young wives are very fond is a piece of buck's skin tied across the chest and falling down to the knees; the more brass buttons sewed to it the better. On marriage or other hilarious occasions, both sexes deck themselves with all the finery obtainable.

CHAPTER VII.

DIFFICULTIES ENCOUNTERED.

WHEN we began our work at Esidumbini, no sign of civilization was visible. Profound ignorance prevailed in regard to religious truth. I asked a young man, "Who made you?" His reply was, "*Unkulunkulu* (Great-Great)." "Where did Unkulunkulu come from?" "He sprang from a reed on the river's brink." "Where was that river?" "I cannot tell. Some believe it is in Natal, others in Zululand." "Who made the reed from which Unkulunkulu sprang?" "I do not know. Our fathers did not inform us." This was the extent of their theological knowledge. A pamphlet has lately been published in Natal by Dean Green, of the English Church, on the proper name for God in the Zulu language. The conclusion to which he arrives, after a most rigid examination, is that Unkulunkulu, literally "Great-Great," is the best word for God. A large majority of missionaries, both in Natal and Zululand, coincide with his views, and doubtless that will soon come into common use. Uixo, a word of Hottentot origin, has been used quite extensively for many years past. There are Zulus in Natal who believe in an "*Itongo*," a great Spirit from whom all things proceeded.

Great simplicity was required in our teaching. The theme that invariably excited interest was the love of Jesus and his agony on the cross. None other awakened an equal amount of thought and feeling. Had we used denunciatory language, or tried to drive them to a reception of Christianity, we should have defeated our object. Kind, gentle, unwearied persuasion and a firm reliance on divine help are the true weapons of a missionary's warfare.

There were occasional gleams of native shrewdness. A lad of seventeen years, looking at me one Sabbath day with twinkling eyes and a countenance full of animation, put the following question: "Do you say, teacher, that the great King has all power in heaven and on earth?" "Yes," I replied. "Well then, why didn't he take a knob-kerrie and, as the serpent was creeping into the garden, give him a rap on the head and thus save the human family from all its woe?"

For a long time it was impossible to persuade the fathers at Esidumbini to allow their daughters to reside in our family, although we offered good compensation. They said, "You will spoil our girls. If taught your notions and customs they will make us trouble and refuse to marry old men who may have eight or ten wives."

They reasoned correctly, for our teaching did have that effect. The young men in our service could not be induced to put on clothing of European make, not even a shirt, though it might be given to them, lest they should encounter ridicule and be accused of adopting the "new religion." This led one of our missionary brethren to make the quaint but truthful remark: "A shirt is the anxious seat among the Zulus;" for as soon as a young man was seen putting on this first article of civilization and Christianity, he was known to be anxious about his spiritual interests.

Worldly considerations alone brought the natives to our Sabbath services. If a man wished to make a good bargain with us on Monday, he was sure to be at church on Sunday.

When a father was asked to send his boys to the station to be taught, the reply was, "What will you pay me?" One who had been quite a regular attendant on the sanctuary for three years came to me one day, and said, "I am coming to meeting no longer; I get nothing for it."

I thought, one Sabbath morning, after preaching five years and witnessing no conversions, that my words had at last sunk into the heart of one man. His countenance was full of life, and his eyes were not taken from me during the sermon. I had been preaching on the storm of divine displeasure that will overtake all unbelievers. He came to me at the close of the service, and said: "Teacher, I thank you for your discourse to-day. I am so glad a storm is coming, for my garden is all parched up with drought."

The prophet Ezekiel (33: 31) describes accurately my congregation at that time: "And they come unto thee as the people cometh, and they sit before thee as my people, and they hear thy words, but do them not: for with their mouth they show much love, but their heart goeth after their gain."

Dark indeed were the prospects; but Mrs. Tyler, whom no obstacles could dishearten, comforted me with the words: "The darkest hour is just before dawn." She used to remind me of a passage in Hebrews, which my good father desired I should never forget: "For ye have need of patience, that, having done the will of God, ye may receive the promise."

I shall speak without reserve of my wife, now in the "better land," for if I have been useful in any degree in the mission field, I attribute it largely to her unwearied help and wise counsels. Though of a delicate organization, she was to me at all times a tower of strength, inspiring me with hope in the darkest hours, uncomplaining in time of trial, willing to wear herself out that others might be benefited. Not only was she necessary to the happiness of her husband, but to the elevation of the Zulus as well. She preached a part of the gospel I could not preach, reaching the hearts of poor Zulu women as no man could have done.

The joys vouchsafed to missionaries more than counterbalance their sorrows. I am sure that we were never happier in our lives. At all times the bow of God's promise overarched us, and our hearts were buoyed up by the assurance that we were remembered in the prayers of dear relatives and friends in our native land. The promise: "Lo, I am with you," was verified to us, and as we could say, "Lo, we have left all, and have followed thee," those words, "Manifold more in this present time, and in the world to come life everlasting," came to us in all their sweetness.

One thing I could not fail to perceive in the early days of our missionary life was that the consciences of the people were on our side. However absorbed in their worldly schemes, however corrupt their inclinations, however closely wedded to their debasing customs, their consciences were responsive to our teaching and testified that the Word we preached was truth. We had abundant evidence that conscience among a heathen people is a great auxiliary to the missionary. I once asked several old men how they felt before the arrival of white men in Zululand, when doing right or wrong. Their reply was, "Something within us approved when we did the former, and condemned when we did the latter." A good commentary this, I thought, on the words of the apostle Paul: "These, having no law, are a law unto themselves; in that they show the work of the law written in their hearts, their conscience bearing witness therewith, and their thoughts one with another accusing or else excusing" (R. V.).

CHAPTER VIII.

TOILING AND WAITING.

OUR chapel, holding about a hundred, was filled every pleasant Sabbath. There was no direct opposition except from a cunning "spirit doctor," who, fearing his craft was in danger, warned the people against having anything to do with us lest the spirits should become angry.

A change was going on silent but sure. The hearts of the natives were being unlocked by sympathy and love. Our arguments against their evil ways were met with a manliness that commanded respect. Though baffled in disputation, they retired from the field with great politeness and grace. We did not see it at the time, but the divine Spirit was working by our side. "Esidumbini for Christ" was our motto, and the Master approved it. He was fertilizing what had been sown in tears.

We used to think at times that friends at home might doubt the expediency of supporting missionaries, year after year, in such an unpromising field.

Mrs. Tyler, in reviewing those early days, once wrote in regard to them: —

"I remember the despair which crept over me when I made my first entrance into a heathen kraal. Everything was so dark and repulsive, it did not seem possible that the pure, genial light of the gospel could find a place there. But it would not do to give way to doubt or despair with the divine promises in our hands. We gathered courage from the bright faces and pleasant smiles with which all greeted us as their first white visitors. To the extent of our ability we answered their questions and interested ourselves in their children, showing them that we were their true friends.

"But when we tried to explain why we had left our native land and come to live with them as messengers of Jesus Christ, silence was the result. Such was the beginning. But when we secured some of the children to work for us, though they knew nothing of our intentions we spent much time in teaching them to repeat passages of Scripture, hoping that these would remain in their hearts, even if they went back to their kraals, and that the Holy Spirit would make use of this instrumentality for their conversion. As soon, however, as some of the parents found that their children were becoming interested in learning they hastened to remove them. This was the disheartening part of our first work, and little understood by expectant Christians and churches."

Subsequently some of the fathers, polygamists, convinced that the religion we taught was true, remarked to me, as did an old Brahman to Dr. Henry M. Scudder, missionary in India, and in almost the identical words: "It is only a question of time, sir. Let us alone. Our children are yours; they will certainly become Christians."

At last our hopes were raised by one of the young men in our employ, Dambusa by name. He came to me, saying, "I believe in Christ and wish to serve him." He had an amiable disposition and was attached to us, but was easily influenced and soon found there was much to contend against. Unfortunately he was engaged to a girl who had no sympathy with him in his desire to embrace Christianity. To make things harder the parents of both were determined to keep their children in heathenism. A house which Dambusa began to build on the station was torn to pieces by indignant relatives. They swore by the spirits of the Zulu kings that none of their number should abandon the worship of their forefathers. The time for the marriage came, the cattle had been paid for, beer brewed, new songs for the dance learned, and Dambusa, almost persuaded, with a sad countenance bade us good-by and joined his heathen friends; but the "incorruptible seed" had been sown in his heart. We shall have more to say of him.

Our heathen congregations were quite orderly. Only once was there an attempt at disturbance. A young man who had, perhaps, imbibed too freely of native beer decided one Sabbath morning to break up our service. I saw in his countenance that mischief was brew-

ing; but he kept quiet till I had commenced
the long prayer, when he began to laugh
aloud and talk to others. Immediately I
stopped praying, and taking him by the nape
of the neck walked him to the door of the
church and gave him a vigorous push which
sent him sprawling out on the ground. I then
returned and resumed my prayer. Occasionally we had lively episodes. The cries of little
babies on their mothers' backs sometimes almost
drowned my voice, but I never asked mothers
to leave the church on that account. One
Sunday a man walked into church carrying a
beaver hat, of which he was very proud; the
gift of some European. It was his only article
of civilized dress. He seated himself, the hat
by his side, and had listened attentively to the
introductory exercises, when a hen took occasion to walk in, fly up, and lay an egg on one
of the boards overhead. The egg rolled one
side and fell directly into his beloved hat.
Zulus have a great repugnance to eggs. They
will not touch one unless obliged. The man's
indescribable disgust as he rose, took up his hat
at arm's length, and walked out of the chapel,
completely upset the gravity of the audience.
He did not return to service that day.

At the Umtwalume station, Saturday evening, a young man, having decided to abandon
heathenism, called on Mr. Wilder, the missionary, and asked for a shirt. He said, "I want
a long one that will cover my knees." The
sewing machine was brought into use, and in a

short time the man had the satisfaction of putting on his first article of civilized clothing. On Sabbath morning he did not take his seat with the unclad heathen in the back part of the chapel, but in front of the pulpit. The bench he occupied had no back, and to make the most of his new garment he raised his feet and pulled his shirt over his knees. He remained in this attitude until, a fit of drowsiness coming over him, he began to sway to and fro, unconsciously attracting general attention. The people, however, retained their gravity until he rolled over like a ball on the floor. Then the risibles of missionary as well as natives became uncontrollable.

CHAPTER IX.

WILD ANIMALS.

BETWEEN Esidumbini and Mapumulo, the station of Rev. Andrew Abraham, lay an immense jungle, in which elephants, buffaloes, leopards, hyenas, and other wild animals lived in comparative security. Only a few hunters had ventured to go into it. Occasionally elephants came out into the open country, but being harassed by Zulus, some of whom had firearms, they were glad to get back to their retreat. Buffaloes, more bold, emerged in droves and grazed within sight of my house. They differ from American buffaloes, or bisons, having a hairless skin, and are more like huge swine. Their horns are generally curved. I once came upon a drove unexpectedly which ran away pellmell, breaking down young trees and everything that impeded their progress. Hunting them is dangerous sport. Baldwin, a great African hunter, used to fear this kind of game more than any other. A narration of his narrow escapes once made my blood run cold.

I had numerous opportunities to try my skill and courage in shooting these animals, but concluded that prudence was the better part of valor. I could not refuse, however, lending my gun to a native hunter, that he might supply himself and friends with food; but a sad accident put a stop to this.

The one I refer to was Umbulawe, who had lived with the Dutch and engaged in many a hunt; but one day a cunning bull buffalo was too much for him. He had fired once and was reloading, when suddenly the bull rushed out of the thicket, knocked him over with his horns, trod upon him, and with his rasp-like tongue tore off a part of his scalp. The poor man held in his breath, pretending to be dead and keeping as still as a mouse, until the savage beast, concluding that life was extinct, walked away. He did not go, however, until he had trampled upon and broken the stock of the gun into half a dozen pieces.

Umbulawe picked himself up as well as he could and soon a party of his friends, who had heard the report of the gun, met him and carried him home. A few hours after his wife came to me with a sad countenance bringing the broken parts of the gun, and said, "Umbulawe is dead." It turned out, however, that the hunter had yet a little life remaining in him and that he was anxious to see me. Taking some sticking-plaster and a few medicines, I mounted my horse, and in twenty minutes rode into his kraal. He was spitting blood and in great pain, and had, I feared, sustained severe internal injuries. Having doctored him according to the best of my ability and given him some advice, I was about to depart when he said, "I want you to make haste and get that gun mended. I must go and shoot that buffalo; he is my enemy." In spite of his injuries Umbulawe recovered in a few weeks.

An Englishman, hunting buffaloes in one of the forests of Zululand, was chased by one, caught on the horns by the strong hunting-belt he had around his waist, and thrown into the branches of a friendly tree to which he gladly clung. The buffalo ran about, apparently in a quandary as to where his game had gone. After ten minutes or more the beast departed, and the tired hunter only regretted that he had not with him his gun that he might give him a farewell charge.

Lions, in considerable numbers, lived on the table-lands, about our station, but rarely came into the Esidumbini valley. One ventured to visit our premises in the night, passing by the front door and walking up to a house occupied by some Zulu lads in my employ. Their door being ajar and one of the boys not asleep, the "fire coming from the lion's nostrils," as he expressed it, so scared him that he roused his companions and they climbed upon the rafters, where they remained till nearly morning. The lion then went past the cattle fold, greatly terrifying the oxen and cows. I noticed that the oxen had made a ring, the cows being inside, that they might protect the weaker sex with their large sharp horns. In the open *veldts*, or plains of South Africa, I have been told that wild animals have a wholesome fear of attacking such a *laayer*, or fortification; but it should be remembered that ox horns in South Africa are generally long and large, differing greatly from those in Great Britain or America. It is not uncommon to see a pair five and even six feet from tip to tip and correspondingly large. One poor ox was so unfortunate as to have a pair nine feet long. An attempt was made to take it to England, but it died on the voyage.

During the first years of my missionary life lions prowling about my station did not disturb us or the natives, if let alone. The country abounded with antelopes, and on these they grew fat. So long as they did not endanger our lives we thought it best to have as little to do with them as possible.

Riding home one day from a meeting of our mission, accompanied by a native lad who was also mounted, we passed within gunshot of the largest male lion I ever saw; but he did not offer to touch us. Shaking his mane and wagging his long tail he walked leisurely away, much to my relief, for I had no more formidable weapon of defense than a jackknife. Natives afterwards told me that he had been in that locality several weeks. A missionary brother was coming to visit us about that time, and I wrote to him, saying, "There is a lion in the way." The good brother was rather incredulous, but took the precaution to ride on horseback ahead of his wagon and, true enough, found the huge beast in the spot I had described. He was wise enough not to shoot, though he had a loaded rifle on his shoulder, knowing that a wounded lion is a most dangerous character.

One of those brutes inflicted on me a great loss one night, and I was glad that a bullet from an Englishman's rifle soon after terminated his existence. I had sent to a table-land, a few miles from my house, two pole oxen which had been recently inoculated to prevent their dying from lung sickness and were, therefore, in low condition. Both were killed by a lion of enormous strength, judging from his tracks and the fact that with his teeth he broke the bone of one of the oxen's legs. He could not have been hungry, for he ate only a small part of one. Those oxen cost me nearly one hundred dollars. A fine horse strayed away from my station one afternoon and was never found, having probably been eaten by a lion. I was not sorry when the country was rid of lions.

When traveling in the Orange Free State, which was noted as a lion country, I learned the *modus operandi* adopted by Dutch farmers in hunting lions. Half a dozen or more courageous boers ride on horseback as far as they dare towards a lion, some of them fire with their long elephant guns from their horses and then retire immediately, glancing backward, perhaps, to see if they have wounded or killed. If unsuccessful in the first charge, they return and make another. The difficulty is to induce their horses to venture within shooting distance, so great is their dread of the "king of beasts." A Dutchman, on whose word I could rely, told me he had shot nine lions and met with only one accident, which was from the fall of his horse when returning from a hunt.

A Natal colonist, William Leathern, while traveling through the Transvaal, some years ago, was obliged to spend the night in the veldt. He was riding one horse and leading another. After kindling a fire he tied the two horses, tail to tail, allowing them to feed near by. A shower descended, putting out the fire, and he was in deep darkness. Suddenly he heard one of his horses utter a terrible cry, and he perceived within a few feet of himself an enormous lion. He fired at him with his pistol, but in a moment the savage beast was upon him inflicting on his right arm a shocking wound. As his horses were both killed, Mr. Leathern was obliged to walk thirty miles before he could reach a physician and have his arm attended to.

An Englishman, by the name of Brown, while hunting in the Orange Free State, shot a lioness, the ball penetrating the skull; but before the wounded animal died she sprang upon the hunter and killed him. Their dead bodies were found side by side.

Readers of the life and travels of Dr. Livingstone will doubtless recall the narrow escape of that great explorer. He had fired the contents of both barrels of his gun into a lion, and was in the act of reloading when the beast sprang upon him, catching him by the shoulder and shaking him as a cat does a rat. The doctor, in describing his sensations at the time, said: "The shock caused a sort of dreaminess in which there was no sense of pain nor feeling of terror, though quite conscious of all that was happening. It was what patients, partially under the influence of chloroform, describe who see the operation but feel not the knife. The shake annihilated fear and allowed no sense of horror in looking around at the beast. This peculiar state is probably produced in all animals killed by the carnivora. And if so, it is a merciful provision of our benevolent Creator for lessening the pain of death." When the remains of the distinguished explorer were taken to England one of the marks by which they were identified was that caused by the teeth of the lion on his shoulder bone.

Another animal that used to make us visits on dark nights was the leopard. I once found myself a little too near one to be agreeable. Hearing the cries of a fowl that roosted on a tree in front of our dwelling, I rushed out, armed with only a broomstick, to see what was the matter. Suddenly I found myself only a yard or two from a large spotted leopard busily eating the fowl. But the greatest terror must have seized him at my ghostlike appearance; for, leaping over a high pomegranate fence, he made off as fast as possible. Leopards often came for sheep and goats which on cold and rainy nights had not been driven to the kraals;

and in such cases I poisoned them for the natives with strychnine, always receiving the skins for my trouble.

Other wild animals to which it was necessary to give a wide berth were wild dogs. They usually go in troops, and if hungry, like Siberian wolves, attack human beings. Should an ox or cow, on account of lameness or disease, be unable to reach the cattle fold before dark, those animals were almost sure to find it. Dr. Adams, riding one night in an unfrequented part of the colony to visit a patient, was chased by a troop of these creatures. At last he turned and rode towards them, cracking his horsewhip furiously and succeeded thus in intimidating them.

Troops of baboons lived on a large table-land lying between Esidumbini and Umsunduzi, a station occupied by Rev. L. Grout, and as I often rode over to see that brother I almost invariably came in contact with them; but we got to understand each other so well that I had no fear and they seemed to be of the same mind. Occasionally, for amusement, I would try to show them how brave I could be and ride on my horse to within a few yards of them. An old baboon, the father and apparently ruler of the colony, would mount on an ant-heap, four or five feet high, and carefully watch my proceedings. If he suspected mischief, — saw anything in my hands that looked like firearms, — he would make a signal to all the mothers and little baboons to flee to their homes on a precipice near by. But if not, he kept quiet, and we exchanged grimaces and remarks also; I addressing him now in English and now in Zulu, and he me in his baboon dialect. Not for the world would I have provoked an attack from him, for I would have stood no chance unless well armed. A large, valuable dog ventured one day to assail one of these fellows and was torn almost to pieces. Natives frequently came to me to borrow my gun, saying that baboons were robbing their gardens. At early dawn, before the people had come out of their huts, a foraging party of these animals would make a raid into a garden, pluck the ears of corn nearly ripe, place them under their arms, steal a pumpkin or two and run away to their hiding-place among the rocks.

Emin Holub, in his "Seven Years in South Africa," tells us that on the highlands he was once pelted by a herd of baboons perched among the trees. He said he had to shoot an old male that began to pick up some stones to throw at him. Members of the same family, living on the lowlands, have not attained to such a degree of intelligence as to defend themselves in that fashion. Certainly they are far removed from those North African specimens, of which Emin Pasha told Mr. Stanley, "that understand the art of fire-making and carry torches at night when they visit the plantations of the Mswa to steal fruit." The Pasha said he had seen this with his own eyes. If blind or nearly so, as he is represented to be, his vision of baboon fire-makers must have been extremely dim.

Naturalists, I believe, class these creatures under the family of "pig-faced baboons;" but their countenances seemed too human to deserve such an appellation. I never had the heart to shoot one, lest his dying struggles should appear to me in my midnight dreams.

At the present time very few wild animals are found in Natal. Occasionally a leopard is killed, but elephants, lions, and wild dogs have disappeared.

CHAPTER X.

CROCODILES AND SNAKES.

AN object of terror to the early missionaries in Natal, when the bridgeless and boatless rivers were swollen, was the crocodile family. I say crocodile, for no alligators are found in South Africa. Travelers generally forded rivers on horseback or in ox-wagons. The loud crack of the whip and shouting of the driver intimidated these reptiles and kept them at safe distance; but a person on foot or on horseback was liable to be seized.

Mr. J. A. Butler, a printer, connected with the American Mission, once had a marvelous escape. He was swimming his horse over a turbid stream, when the animal became frightened and he discovered that a huge crocodile had hold of him. The scaly brute, leaving the horse, seized the rider, dragged him from his saddle and would have made him his prey had not Mr. Butler clung to the horse's mane. When he reached the bank of the river, he caught hold of some reeds and held on to them until a party of Zulus, who had witnessed the exciting scene, rushed to his relief. Even then the brute would not relax his hold, till the natives had beaten him on the head with clubs and pried open his jaws. They then helped Mr. Butler out, bound up his wounds, and accompanied him to the nearest mission station, six miles distant. The poor man recovered, but was a sufferer from the wounds he received the rest of his life.

Escapes from a crocodile, after he has fairly seized one, are rare, but sometimes occur. It is reported that an Englishman while bathing was drawn by one into deep water; but having been told that crocodiles are sensitive about their eyes, he thrust his fists into them, and the reptile not fancying this treatment let go his hold. The man, though badly lacerated, lived many years.

A laughable story is told by George Cato, Esq., American Consul at Port Natal, of Potgeiter Dorse, a Dutchman. Dorse, while hunting, decided to have a bath in the Umhlali River. Leaving his clothing on the river's bank, together with his gun and hunting-knife, he engaged peacefully in his ablutions; but when he had finished he did not find the clothes where he had left them. Crocodile tracks explained the matter and soon he obtained sight of the thief on a sand bank a few yards away. Taking good aim he gave him a fatal shot in the brain. Then with his knife he opened the brute, secured his clothes, none the worse apparently for the mangling they had received, put them on and went home.

William Baldwin, in his book on "African

Hunting," tells us of shooting several geese which disappeared as soon as they were shot, being drawn under water by some unseen creature. Determined to secure at least one, he waded into the pond and caught hold of it by the legs just as it was sinking, a crocodile having taken the first hold. He observes: "In an instant the goose came in halves, the legs and back falling to my share, Mr. Alligator getting the best half and two or three violent blows on the nose into the bargain." He adds, "I lost not an instant in getting ashore again and did not think much at the time of what a foolish thing it was to do and what a narrow escape I had had."

Dr. Livingstone speaks of the Barotzi tribe, living on the Zambezi, as inclined to pray to these reptiles and to eat them too; but the Zulus manifest no disposition to do either. They use various parts of the body, however, for medicinal purposes. If one of the Bamangwato people has the misfortune to be bitten by a crocodile, he is expelled from his tribe. Dr. Livingstone said that he met with a man in exile who refused to tell him the cause, but some of his native attendants informed him, and the scars visible on his thigh attested the truth of their assertion.

South Africa is emphatically a land of snakes. They are so common, and the stories told of them are so exaggerated, that strangers coming to the colony are in terror of them for months. An Englishman, who had landed in

Natal a week or two before, stopped one night
at my house. Upon retiring he searched his
room carefully for the possible snake he might
find lurking in some corner. Seeing what he
supposed to be a deadly serpent he rushed
out and insisted that I should call some one
to assist me in killing the creature. Four
native boys armed with knob-kerries and canes,
and eager for the fray, went into the room;
but after long searching found only the cover
of a pail which had been pushed into the
corner.

Serpents very rarely attack a human being,
except in self-defense. There is much truth
in the following statement taken from a Natal
paper: —

"Nearly all the wounds inflicted by venomous
snakes upon men are the result of the want of
a frank understanding between the parties.
The gentleman inadvertently sets his foot on
the reptile's tail, and the reptile, under the impression that the insult was premeditated, re-
sents the action; or the gentleman has a
friend who wishes for a green snake to put in
a bottle and endeavors to induce some slippery
individual of the race to the bottling condition,
while the snake, knowing nothing of the honor
of the embalmment for which he is marked out,
does his best to give his assailant 'pause,' in
order that he may take himself out of the
way during the cessation of the strife."

Many of the harmless snakes in South
Africa so resemble the poisonous ones that

it is often difficult to distinguish them. It would hardly be safe for a person in Natal to imitate the author of Pilgrim's Progress, of whom it is said in his memoir that, "One day an adder crossed his path and after stunning it with his stick, he opened its mouth and with his fingers plucked out its fangs," by which act he says, "Had not God been merciful to me, I might by my desperateness have brought myself to my end." English adders cannot be handled with impunity, much less African.

The largest serpent in South Africa is the python, or Natal rock snake. No true boa constrictors are found in Africa, their habitat being South America, India, the Moluccas, Cuba, and Australia. Du Chaillu speaks of a python in Equatorial Africa measuring over thirty-three feet in length. In the southern part of the continent I never heard of one more than twenty-three feet, and the longest I ever saw was twenty-one feet. If attacked, a python will wind itself about a human being and crush him to death; but for food it usually prefers small mammalia, such as conies, rabbits, etc.

Mr. Thomas Baines, a traveler and artist in South Africa, relates an incident he received from a Dutch boer. "One of these pythons finding a native asleep began to swallow him, but commencing at the wrong end, and taking only one foot into his mouth, was unable to draw him farther than the fork, and then, endeavoring to eject the limb, was prevented by his crooked fangs sticking in the flesh. The native awakening screamed lustily, but no help came, and his leg remained a whole day and night in the snake's throat before help arrived to set him free."

A sportsman in Natal once found a python asleep and disturbed its slumber by a charge of buckshot. After repeated contortions the creature straightened itself out and appeared to be dead. Wishing to save its skin, the sportsman offered his native servant a reward if he would carry it to his home. As he was reluctant to do so, on the ground that the serpent was only "pretending to be dead," the master took it up and carried it a little way himself. The native then mustered courage to shoulder the reptile, but soon shouted to his master, "*Nkosi ngi size* (Master, help me)!" The python had put his teeth into the native's thigh and was lashing its tail violently in various directions for a stump or stone to which to fasten itself. Had not the sportsman rushed to his help, the poor Zulu might have had an uncomfortable, if not fatal, squeeze.

The largest python I ever saw was brought to me by a party of Zulus who had found it attempting to swallow an antelope. The horns were too spreading to be disposed of, and the serpent was robbed of its meal by the natives, who immediately feasted upon the venison, and brought the snake to me. The creature measured eighteen feet, and was the longest I ever skinned. So great is the vitality of the python that I once saw one wriggling its tail several hours after it had been killed.

In his "Curiosities of Natural History," Frank Buckland relates that two pythons, one nine and the other eight feet in length, were kept in a box in the Zoölogical Gardens in London. One morning the keeper found the shorter serpent missing, and on examination noticed that the longer one was greatly distended, having swallowed his companion. As the Zulus believe that the spirits of their ancestors take up their abode in serpents they never eat them, as do some tribes in Central Africa.

The puff adder is a much-dreaded snake, owing to its habit of lying in frequented paths and its resemblance to pieces of decayed wood. In Cape Colony they are often seen as large as a man's arm, and a bite from an adder is difficult to cure. One day a little son of Mr. Lindley came upon a large adder, and, though a boy only six years old, he took off his shoe and killed it; then seizing it by the tail he dragged it home.

A cry dreaded by natives and white people alike is that of "*Imamba! Imamba!*" especially if the word *emyama* (black) is added. The imambas are slender snakes of a vivid green or black color, the latter being by far the more dangerous and dreaded serpent. If one enters a Zulu hut, the greatest consternation prevails, and no native will try to kill one unless he is well armed. Calling early one morning on a sugar planter, whom I found at his mill, we were suddenly surprised by the appearance of a servant, highly excited, saying, "The mistress needs you; there is a snake in her bedroom!" We hastened to the house and saw a huge imamba, which had just been killed by an Indian coolie. It had crawled into the bedroom and concealed itself in a manilla hat, near the head of the bed. When the good housewife went to make the bed she saw his serpentship coiled up in the hat, but had sufficient presence of mind to keep quiet until her servant could inflict a fatal blow. The planter told me that he had felt something creeping over his body in the night, but was too sleepy to ascertain the cause. Had he been bitten, instant death would have ensued.

The green imamba, though not so dangerous, is more common. A missionary sent a native into the garden for a bunch of bananas. The boy did his errand, bringing the bananas to the house on his head. As he put down the bunch, an imamba slowly uncoiled itself from the fruit. The native, it was said, turned almost white on seeing the danger to which he had been exposed.

A story is told of a gentleman in India, who was so disturbed by a noise under the floor of his room that he cut a hole through and baited a hook with a toad. Seeing the line move he pulled it up and found he had a poisonous snake.

Once I was exceedingly annoyed by the noise made by some rats over my head. Suddenly all became quiet and I supposed a cat had found its way above the ceiling. I ascertained soon after that instead of a cat it was a snake.

That snakes are famous rat-catchers I had evidence another time. My stable, after having been overrun with rats, was all at once entirely free from them. A few days afterwards my son was standing in the stable and saw an imamba, ten feet long, coiled about a beam a few yards above his head. A shot ended his existence, and two days later the mate was also disposed of.

It is not unusual to see these creatures moving along the branches of trees in search of weaver birds' nests, and I have frequently seen one put its long slender neck into the hanging nest to enjoy its feast of young birds. The parent birds in the meantime utter most pathetic cries, but are helpless before their enemy.

One of the pioneer missionaries showed great courage and nerve-force one Sabbath. During the sermon a green imamba moved along and coiled itself on a beam just above the preacher's head. The sermon was finished and prayer and benediction pronounced before the order to kill the snake was given.

Another missionary, hearing a rustling in his room one night after retiring, found an imamba moving about and killed it. Very soon he was again disturbed and found the mate to the first snake.

Zulus do not swish the air with rods, or rub the soles of their feet with garlic, to keep snakes at a distance as do the natives of Western Africa, but they sometimes use tobacco for this purpose. Serpents will not enter a hut which has a strong odor of the "filthy weed." Should one show more vitality than is agreeable after receiving fatal wounds, a Zulu will sometimes pry open its jaw and insert a little snuff, and its contortions cease almost instantly.

The chief remedy I have found successful for snakebites is ammonia; though some use ipecacuanha. Fresh milk, if given immediately after a bite, is said to be a good antidote, but I never tried it. The natives use the root of the yellow daphne. It is said that toads bitten are seen hopping to the *umuti wenhlangwana*, the herb used as an antidote for the bite of a serpent, called *inhlangwana*. It is marvelous that so few people are fatally bitten, considering how numerous serpents are. I have never heard of a missionary having lost his life in this way.

CHAPTER XI.

SPIRIT WORSHIP.

IT is often said that "Zulus are snake worshipers." This is not strictly true. *Amatongo* (ancestral spirits) are the objects of their worship. When the body dies, the *umoya* (soul, or spirit) is supposed to take up its abode in a snake, or to assume the form of this reptile. An intelligent Zulu, not a Christian, thus explains the belief of his countrymen on this subject: —

"We believe that there are good and evil spirits; the good ones watching over us for good, and the evil ones ready to do us harm. Some spirits, the good ones, those of our families, who are interested in our welfare, are allowed to assume the form of a certain snake, and by that means not only form a link between us and the world of spirits, but in the guise of a snake they are permitted thus to watch over us. We believe in the spirit the snake represents."

The soul of a king or any distinguished person is represented by the imamba, a fierce and venomous serpent, surpassed only by the python in size and length. Common people assume the form of harmless and quiet serpents. To kill an itongo (spirit), or rather its serpent representative, is a crime to be atoned for immediately, lest some dire calamity result. An ox or cow must be slaughtered; blood must be shed. "Without shedding of blood there is no remission." Immediately after death the graves of Zulu men (not of women, except in the case of a queen) are fenced about, covered with thorns, and closely watched for weeks, sometimes for months, lest a witch or poisoner disturb the remains. Should the watcher happen to see a snake among the thorns, he would remark to his friends, "I saw the spirit of our father to-day basking in the sun on the top of his grave." Were he kind and gentle when alive, he would probably add: "We need not fear, he will still treat us in the same way he did when alive."

Dr. Henry M. Callaway, in conversation with the natives, obtained the following information: —

When sickness invades a kraal, the oldest son praises the spirit of his father or grandfather, giving him the names he has gained by valor in battle. He sometimes chides as well as praises, especially if the sickness seems likely to terminate fatally, saying, "If we should all die in consequence of the affliction you are sending upon us, your worshipers will come to an end; therefore, for your own sake as well as ours, do not destroy us."

When a family moves to another part of the country and does not see in the new place the snake representing the paternal spirit, they conclude that it has remained behind and return to sacrifice an ox, giving thanks and singing the same songs the father sang when alive. This they maintain is to excite pity, so that he may say: "Truly, my children are lonely because they do not see me." If a widow left with small children neglects them, the spirit of the departed husband is likely to appear to her in a dream, saying, "Why have you left my children? Go back to them. If you do not, I will kill you." The command is generally heeded.

Zulu ancestral spirits are not free from jealousy. When an animal is sacrificed by the headman of a kraal to appease the spirits and avert death, he will go outside the cattle enclosure and pray as follows: "All hail, spirits of our tribe! Is it proper, instead of asking for food, that you should come to us at all times in the form of sickness? No, it is proper if you demand food that I should not refuse it. There, then," pointing to the slaughtered animal, "is your food. All ye spirits of our tribe, summon one another! I am not going to say, So-and-so, there is your food, for you are jealous. I give you what you ask. Let the man get well."

Were there certain imperfections on the body of a man while living; had he for instance but one eye or did he go lame, the serpent representative is sure to resemble him.

Zulus sometimes connect shadows with spirits. They say, "The shadow that is cast by the body will ultimately become the itongo, or spirit, when the body dies." A missionary, wishing to get at the meaning of the above, inquired, "Is the shadow which my body casts when I am walking my spirit?" The reply was, "No; it is not your itongo (guardian spirit watching over you), but it will be the itongo for your children when you are dead." Long shadows, they say, shorten as men approach the end of life. At death the observation is, "The shadow hath departed." A short shadow, however, remains with the dead body and is buried with it. The long shadow becomes an itongo.

Vows to sacrifice to the spirits are frequently made by Zulus. If a child is ill and the diviner has not been consulted, the father addresses the spirits thus: "If it is you, people of our house, who are doing this, I make a vow: behold, there is such and such a bullock! Let the child get well, that you may eat;" or, if he does not possess a bullock, the father cries, "If you wish for food, why do you not cure my child, that I may go and get you a bullock and kill it for you that you may eat? How shall I know it is you if the child does not get well?"[1]

Enough has been said to show that ancestral spirits are the objects of Zulu worship, and the same may be said of native tribes generally in South Africa. Their influence not only

[1] See Callaway, on "Ancestor Worship."

Spirit Worship. 97

over individuals, but over all mundane affairs, is, in the estimation of the heathen, incalculably great. The nature of that influence depends on their disposition, for they can be benevolent or malevolent—guardian angels sweet and kind, or cruel and destructive. They can make crops productive or blast them; can cause health and prosperity, or send disease and death. Before going to war it has been a Zulu custom, from time immemorial, to send individuals into the enemy's country to steal a child, who is offered as a sacrifice to the spirits to obtain their favor and insure victory. If successful, the blood of oxen and goats flows freely from their altars, and their thanksgivings are profuse.

In reference to the locality of the departed spirits, the natives universally say, "It is *pansi* (regions under the earth)." The manner in which they obtained a knowledge of Hades is given to us in one of their traditions. A hunter chased a deer into a deep hole made by an ant-bear, and following it he descended deeper and deeper till he came to the abode of his ancestors. On his return he reported an abundance of cattle, all white, and food in sufficient quantity. Indeed, the subterraneans were in good circumstances. The number of those who place any faith in this tradition is few. Deeply conscious of a future state, most of them have fearful forebodings of what may befall them in that state. A Zulu man once said to me as he was about to die, "I am sinking into a dark deep pit. I am afraid." He expressed the feeling of benighted Africans generally. Their religion, if spirit worship can be called religion, affords no comfort in a dying hour. For many years I watched carefully the workings of the native mind in times of trouble. It is then they apply to the spirits for aid. Healthy and strong, with food in abundance, and that of the most nutritious kind, naturally vivacious and cheerful in temperament, reveling in the excitement of the hunt, the dance, beer party, or carousal over the slaughtered ox, they are as happy as barbarians can be. Unrestrained in body or mind they enjoy life in their salubrious climate to a great degree. Smiles are generally seen on their faces, and it is doubtful whether a more social people can anywhere be found; but when visited by affliction their deepest passions are excited. In case of death the headman of the kraal looks up and around him and says, "This is mysterious. We shall all die if something is not done." In many cases the disease is unknown or it baffles the skill of physicians, which is not strange, for Zulu "medicine men," in attempting to save life, as frequently destroy it by cramming down a multitude of drugs without stopping to watch the effect of one. The afflicted man fixes his suspicion on some individual with whom he has been at variance, but having no clew which would satisfy the minds of others he calls the people together. The attendance is usually

Spirit Worship.   99

large, for the neighbors fear lest their absence be construed into an indication of guilt. With grave countenances they seat themselves in a circle on the ground, and after the usual salutation and passing round the snuffbox, the troubled individual begins his speech: "Men, friends! to-day you see me in grief. You all know I am a man of peace. I have wronged no one. I have eaten my own food and attended to my own business; but an enemy is plotting my ruin. My brother has been suddenly taken away. A wizard is destroying us. Tell me what I must do." The replies are guarded, but all unite in the opinion that no time should be lost or expense begrudged in applying to a diviner and through him to the spirit world, that the foul deed may be traced to its source.

The character and functions of Zulu diviners, or spirit doctors, may be briefly described. Various names are given to them. One is *izinyanga zokubula* (doctors of smiting), because great use is made of canes in smiting the ground by those who consult them. Another is *izanusi* (smellers out), or discoverers of criminals and those possessed with witchcraft, believed to be in communication with the amatongo.

The diviners work powerfully on the superstitions of their countrymen. That they may become thoroughly acquainted with their art, they endure a great amount of self-sacrifice. For instance, they leave their homes, isolate themselves from their fellows, live and sleep in solitary places, fraternize with wild animals, endure hunger and cold and talk to the moon until they become almost, if not quite, lunatic.

Their clothing is hideous, consisting of skins of crocodiles and pythons, with the teeth of wild cats and fetiches of various kinds about their necks, the bladders of birds and wild beasts on their heads, and a long leopard's skin dangling about their loins.

They formerly possessed unlimited power over their deluded countrymen. One visited an American mission station in Natal and warned those who had nominally embraced Christianity that if they remained longer under the influence of the white teacher they would all die. Terrified and weak in the faith many left at once, some never to return.

Having observed closely the izanusi while in the process of calling up the spirits, shouting "*Yizwa! yizwa!* (Hear! hear!)" while the seated consulters beat the ground with their canes, and having listened to the ambiguous oracles delivered to the ignorant and credulous, I have not wondered that the people are deceived.

These crafty izanusi do not go into Hades for nothing. A large fat ox is generally the reward and often a goat besides. If not satisfied, they say to the people, "Give me something to wipe my eyes with," which means that they are unable to see clearly, that they have not been properly compensated.

It is a matter of thanksgiving that in various parts of South Africa the "smelling out" of individuals (pronouncing them witches) is prohibited and a great amount of bloodshed prevented through the intervention of British authority. May the time soon come when it will cease entirely!

It is said that Chaka, who ruled in Zululand at the beginning of this century, once had the courage to charge all the izanusi in his kingdom with being humbugs. During the night he sprinkled blood about the royal kraal and called the doctors to investigate the cause. One smelt out this person, another that. Only one guessed rightly, saying, "I smell out the heavens" (meaning the king). His life was spared; all the rest were killed.

Protracted and patient instruction will be needed ere native Christians are wholly emancipated from the idea that the ancestral spirits are able to avert evil and that the izanusi have dealings with them. I had occasion to discipline two church members of several years' standing for uniting secretly with their heathen friends in sacrificing an ox to the spirit of their father; the "doctor" having told them they would die if they refused. Remove the deep-seated superstitious regard Zulus have for their departed relatives and their faith in their doctors of divination, and the keystone in the arch of their religion will be gone.

From what has been said, it is evident that "spirit doctors" discharge a sacerdotal function, offering up sacrifices for which their mercenary spirit leads them to demand good pay. In propitiatory sacrifices they usually have a part. It is exceedingly touching to observe the reverential attitude and listen to the apparently sincere and fervent supplications of the aged men when engaged in their sacrifices. S. O. Samuelson, Esq., thus speaks of them: —

"Beautiful and seemingly heartfelt prayers are offered up to the spirits when the animal is killed, thanking them for all the mercies, attention, protection, and care of the past, and invoking a continuance of the same. The weakness, helplessness, and worthlessness of humanity are acknowledged and an entire dependence on the spirits and their good offices confessed. The prayer offered up occupies some time, both before and after the animal is killed, and is very interesting to those who understand the native language. . . . When the headman of a kraal performs the sacrificial rite he first selects an animal, and then, with the male members of the kraal, goes into the cattle enclosure into which the victim for sacrifice has been previously brought. He then engages in a long earnest prayer to the spirits, holding the assegai specially reserved for such occasions in his hand. The prayer sets forth the weakness, dependence, and poverty of the human race, and supplicates guidance, strength, health, plenty, and security from those who were in their time human and acquainted with grief, but now are in a better position and who alone can give necessary relief. After the prayer he hands the assegai to one of his attendants to stab the ox. A short prayer follows, asking the spirits to accept favorably the sacrifice. The blood flowing from the wound is received into vessels ready for the purpose, each hut bringing its own special vessel, while there is one for the whole kraal. It is used the next day for a special dish, of which the natives are very fond, called *ububende*, consisting of small portions of meat, fat, and entrails minced up and boiled in the blood. A portion of the caul is set fire to and taken from hut to hut in a burning state as a pleasant incense to the spirits, the headman at the same time uttering a prayer for peace and prosperity to the inmates. The gall bladder is cut out and its contents sprinkled on the children and on himself, with a prayer to the spirits that the young may enjoy health and prosperity and that he may live to witness it. The meat is roasted or boiled within the cattle fold by the men. No females are allowed to go within the enclosure, but meat is sent to them where they are sitting near their huts."

CHAPTER XII.

SUPERSTITIONS OF THE ZULUS.

ZULU superstitions are legion. For a turkey buzzard to light on a hut, for a cony to run into a kraal, for a toad to jump into a fireplace, is ominous of evil. The bleating of a sheep while being slaughtered is a bad omen. If a cow push off with her horns the lid of a dish that holds Indian corn or other grain, it is a sign that some calamity will happen.

No one dares to drink sour milk during a thunderstorm, and no woman ventures to work in the garden the day after a hailstorm. A fowl must never be carried through a field when the corn is tasseling out, lest the crop be blighted. Should a garden be in an unhealthy state, fish skin, the salter the better, is burned and the ashes scattered over the ground to cure diseases which are supposed to hinder vegetation.

Various ceremonies are performed on infants, and fathers are not allowed to see their own babies until their little heads have been smoked and they have undergone other absurd processes. If twins are born, one is immediately destroyed lest the father die. They justify this habit, saying it is better for the mother and for the remaining child; but this superstition

is the true reason. The Zulus have great faith
in certain medicines and often wear charms or
fetiches to ward off diseases and protect them
from enemies. One is often seen biting off a
bit of root from a piece suspended about his
neck to soften the heart of a person with
whom he wishes to make a bargain. Before
going into battle Zulu warriors drink certain
medicines to make their enemies faint-hearted.
To make dogs serviceable in hunting they are
fed on the beaks and claws of birds. To render
a man brave and successful on a hunting
excursion he must have leopard's whiskers
pounded fine mixed with his food.

The medicine men carry about the wherewithal
to make people love or hate, as suits
their purpose. If a young man finds his love
for a certain damsel unreturned, or suspects
that she prefers another, the doctor can give a
medicine to make her hate the latter and love
the former.

A heathen mother once administered a powerful
emetic to her son, who professed Christianity,
to make him cast up his new religion.

One cold rainy day I was called to examine
the corpse of a native which had been found
several miles from my home. The men who
discovered it feared they might be accused of
murder unless some white man saw the body.
Mounting my horse, I rode to the spot and
finding no marks of violence I had a grave
dug, and called upon some of the twenty or
more men present to deposit the dead man in

his last resting place. Not one of them would budge an inch. I took a small bag of medicines or charms from the pocket of his vest (his only article of clothing) and poured them out on my hand. The greatest consternation was depicted on the faces of the natives. They looked on me very much, I imagine, as did the barbarous Melitans upon Paul when he shook off the "venomous beast" from his hand. I had to pull and roll the dead body into the grave with my own hands and offer a prayer, before they would even cover it with earth. After the ride and exposure in the rain I had a violent chill and I dosed myself vigorously, remarking to my wife that it would never do for me to be sick or die just then, as the natives would believe it to be the effect of the dead man's medicines. I was told afterwards that no reward, however great, would have induced one of them to touch that body.

One of the first missionaries to the Zulus was accustomed to take his overcoat to the place of religious service whenever there was a probability of rain. A drought having come, he was importuned by no means to leave behind his "rain-producing garment."

In speaking to children and showing Zulu curios, I am sometimes asked about idols worshiped by the natives. The Zulus are not image-worshipers. If a Zulu hunter fails to kill for several shots, he will take his gun to a spirit doctor, who after examination usually informs him that his deceased grandfather is angry with

Superstitions of the Zulus.

him. An ox must be slaughtered before the hunting can go on; the gall of the animal is scattered over the bodies of those engaged in the sacrifice and a part of the beef is set aside for the use of the spirit. The messenger of the spirits it is said will come and take it; but it is invariably swallowed by the natives.

The most fearful superstitions are those connected with witchcraft. A Zulu's imagination peoples all Southern Africa with wizards, persons of the most dangerous character who are supposed to wander about and deposit poison in the path or before the kraals of those who are victimized. I once poisoned a hyena which had been stealing my fowls and buried the carcass. Two men came to me in great excitement, begging me to exhume the hyena and let the vultures consume it, lest wizards should take the liver and poison the whole country. I offered them spades to dig it up themselves, but this they were unwilling to do.

Zulus are great believers in dreams. Under their guidance they perform the most absurd ceremonies and do the strangest things. If one who is on a hunting excursion, far from home, should happen to dream that a relative has died, he must abandon the hunt at once and go and see if it be true. If not, he considers it necessary to consult a spirit doctor, who must be paid for his services. Should the information he receives from the spirit world through the doctor confirm his dream, then an ox must be slaughtered as a sacrificial offering.

A man dreams that an attempt has been made to take his life by one whom he always regarded as his true friend. On awaking he says: "This is strange; a man who never stoops to meanness wishes to destroy me. I cannot understand it, but it must be true, for 'dreams never lie.'" Although the suspected friend protests his innocence, he immediately cuts his acquaintance.

If one dreams of being attacked by a buffalo, or some other wild animal, the dreamer inquires, "What have I done that the spirits send a wild beast to kill me?"

If in time of war the dream is of an enemy coming to murder men, women, and children, so terrified are the people that the kraal must be removed at once to a place of safety.

The next dream may be of a serpent coming and saying, "Do you know that when you killed a serpent the other day you knocked in the head of your grandfather who came to visit you?" A fat ox must be slaughtered to appease the offended spirit.

Curious to relate, a Zulu's dream of a wedding or dance is ominous of evil, whereas one of a sick or dead person is a good sign.

It will be long, I fear, before even Christian Zulus are wholly emancipated from the power of superstitious dreams. Listen to one whose reason and piety were struggling against the absurd notions of his people: —

"Of what use will it be if when I pray I am made to arise from my knees by beasts which devour me, when forsooth they are not real? for I cannot get that for which I awake early to pray unto the Lord, being prevented by the beasts which I see. When I was kneeling, there came a snake to do as on other days. I said, No! To-day let me feel by my body that it has already seized me. Then there came a man running to stab me at once. I conquered him. I went home, having ascended a rock of safety, saying, Oh, forsooth, I have been hindered by fantasies!"[1]

Lightning fills the native mind with great fear. It is not uncommon to see on the huts half a dozen or more sticks that have been medicated by "lightning doctors" that no harm may occur. These "doctors" are supposed to possess the power of sending the electric current wherever they choose. Hence the people stand in awe of them. The Zulus believe in a "bird of heaven," which they say comes down during a thunderstorm and is found in localities which have been struck by lightning. The "doctors" watch for the appearance of this bird, kill it, and use its fat to anoint the lightning-sticks on the huts and enable them to act on the heavens without harm to themselves.

Earthquakes are unspeakably awful phenomena to the Zulus. One occurred in Natal, in 1850, shortly after I went to my station. The

[1] Callaway's Dreams of the Zulus.

men, savants of the tribe, assembled from far and near to discuss the cause. Some said it was the English firing off big cannon, fifty miles away. Others, and the larger part, attributed it to the rolling over in his grave of Chaka, an old Zulu king. As they could not agree, the decision was left to the missionary. One morning I perceived in front of my door twenty or more men, delegates sent to inquire about the earthquake. I gave them a brief geological lecture and dismissed them, but I never heard whether they were satisfied.

When an army is about to invade the enemy's country a peculiar custom is observed to ascertain whether victory or defeat will follow. It is that of churning medicines. Two kinds are chosen, one representing their king, the other the enemy. These medicines are placed in separate dishes, and if the one representing the enemy froths up suddenly, whilst that representing the king does not, they regard it as a sign that the enemy will prove too strong for them and the army is not allowed to go out to battle.

Sneezing is regarded by the Zulus as an indication of good health, and immediately after this operation they ejaculate thanks to the spirits of their ancestors. The exclamation often is: "Spirits of our people, grant me long life!" The time spent in sneezing is considered lucky, for then the spirits are more benevolent than at other times. Zulu diviners, it is said, are apt to sneeze freely

Superstitions of the Zulus. 111

when in the process of divination and it is considered a sign that the spirits are present.

When cattle stray away from a Zulu kraal and are lost, a hawk called *isipumunyumanyati*, about the size of a crow, is consulted. If it points its head in a certain direction, searchers are immediately sent towards that point secure in the belief that they will find the lost animals.

S. C. Samuelson, Esq., has recorded a large number of Zulu superstitions, among which are the following:—

"Till of late, and perhaps now in some localities, it has been regarded as sorcery to carry manure into a garden, for if he who does it should have a larger crop than his neighbors suspicions might arise that would lead to his death. Thus they are prevented from fertilizing the soil, and the poor women are constantly obliged to find new places for planting.

"There are certain mountains which are objects of special regard, at which natives dare not point with the extended finger, but with the fist or thumb, lest thunder and hail storms result.

"No one dares to kill a turkey buzzard, lest the arm with which it was done be paralyzed.

"A person afflicted with mumps must go to an ant-bear's hole and shout, '*Uzagiga! uzayiya!* (The mumps! the mumps!).' If he returns home without looking back, the disease will leave him.

"If an otter should be killed in the daytime, it must not be removed until a certain amount of manœuvering is accomplished for fear of a deluge, the otter being a water animal.

"Women, when sowing grain, carry with them the leaves and roots of the *isidwa* (yellow lily), as it is supposed to improve the nutritive qualities of the grain to be produced.

"When a girl reaches a marriageable age, a cow must be slaughtered for her. If not, she will be a barren wife.

"The hair and skin of a hyena, burned, is a powerful remedy for kidney diseases among cattle.

"The crossing of a threshold by a peculiar serpent with a horny spine portends a serious calamity. This serpent is supposed to recover, although its back is broken many times. The spirits restore it. Some hold that the *inhlonhlo*, a species of the imamba family, a very dangerous serpent, cannot possibly be killed.

"According to Zulu belief, any object, a stick or chip or certain spots in the highway, may be so doctored as to cause death when touched by an individual.

"A fabulous animal named *utokoto* is said to exist, which has a special fondness for the flesh of human females.

"Monkeys' tails, according to Zulu belief, originated as follows: — A party of women who were digging in a garden gave chase to a troop of those animals and beat them on their backs with their heavy hoes. Immediately the long tails appeared.

"A class of spirits called *imikovu* is an object of great terror. They are said to be speechless and wandering about in forests. Death is the result of contact with them.

"Natives believe that any one charged with an offense has the power, by eating a certain root, of causing the assembly of men trying him to wander in their minds so that they cannot arrive at a decision."

A kind of divination called *umlingo* is met with among the Zulus. "A native doctor may pour water into a calabash full of small holes, and by this means, observing the direction in which it spouts, he can divine the direction from whence the disease has come upon his patient. Kings have made use of umlingo to divine the probability of success in their undertakings. This was done in several ways. One was to sprinkle hot water on some of the soldiers about to commence their march, and if they were not scalded so that blisters were formed then the enemy would succeed."

Umabope is a climbing plant with red roots, bits of which are worn about the necks by natives for charms. The root is chewed by Zulus for a few minutes when going to battle and then they spit it out in the direction of the enemy. It is believed that the enemy will in consequence commit some foolish act which will lead to destruction.

To quote further from Mr. Samuelson : —

"The custom of 'rendering the army invulnerable,' as it is called, preparatory to its commencing hostile operations against an enemy, takes place in the chief kraal and all the men have to attend. The sacrificial beast is selected by the doctor in charge of the proceedings. The animal is at once caught and thrown down by force. The skin is removed from one shoulder, and it is cut out before the animal is killed. The flesh of the shoulder is cut into long strips, roasted on the coals of a fire prepared for the purpose, into which certain kinds of bitter herbs and roots are thrown by the doctor. The flesh is roasted and made to pass through the smoke arising from this fire. The meat is then ready to be eaten ; each man bites off a mouthful of a strip and passes it on to the next man. When the meat is consumed, the doctor sprinkles the men with water into which has been put some pulverized charcoal of the flesh and medicines I have named. All this while the poor victim has been left to writhe in agony. It is now killed and the flesh consumed. It is publicly eaten by all the men present. All the bones are burned. No females may have any of the flesh of an animal killed for this ceremony.

"The medicine used by the natives in purification after killing any one is called *icima mlilo* (fire-quencher) and it is composed of a variety of ingredients answering very much to this prescription : —

   Tooth of fox and weasel's bone,
   Eye of cat and skull of cat,

And the hooked wing of bat;
Mandrake root and murderer's gore,
Henbane, hemlock, hellebore,
Lithium, storax, bdellium, borax,
Ink of cuttlefish and feather
Of screech owl smoke together.

"A bath is also necessary after the medicine is taken. A native must always go through the process of purification after killing any one, and in case of homicide or murder it would be a most important bit of evidence against any one could it be proved that he had been using the icima mlilo and had taken a bath soon after such a deed was committed.

"There is a class of people, known by the natives as *izinswelaboya*, who are believed to haunt isolated and unoccupied parts of the country where thick mists and fogs are prevalent. They are said to be *abatakati* (miscreants and evil doers of the worst class) who waylay unwary travelers and murder them for the sake of obtaining certain portions of their bodies, such as the heart, which are made use of for medicines and charms. It is believed that many native doctors are in league with these men and give them a good price for such portions of the human body as they consider most valuable. Natives have a great dread of the izinswelaboya, and they dare not travel through districts said to be infested by them after dark or alone. There is good reason, I am afraid, for such a fear, because natives have often disappeared mysteriously and have never been heard of again, whilst some have been found murdered and mutilated in a most cruel manner. Persons murdered by the izinswelaboya are almost invariably found with the tip of the tongue, the eyelids, portions of the ears, and the points of the fingers and toes cut off, in addition to other mutilations. The tip of the tongue is cut off that no tongue can give information of the deed, the eyelids that none may see it, the ears that none may hear it."

CHAPTER XIII.

POLYGAMY AND OTHER EVIL PRACTICES.

POLYGAMY presents a gigantic obstacle to the elevation of the Zulus. It has been well called their "idol and their curse." The chattelizing of women is its twin sister. All that a Zulu man hath will he give for wives, and the number he possesses is limited only by the number of cows he has with which to buy them. Wives and cattle are his property and a Zulu is not considered of much importance unless enriched with a large number of the former. "A man's wives make the house great" is a common Zulu saying. With only one wife a man is considered poor. "If I have but one wife, who will cook for me when she is ill?" is a question often asked by the wife-loving Zulu when arguing in support of his darling custom. In Natal for some years the market price for a strong, healthy girl of fifteen years ranged from fifteen to twenty cows, but of late ten have been considered the standard price. As the colonial law now stands, no Zulu father can collect in court of justice more than that number for his daughter. Hereditary chiefs and constables, however, are exceptions. They can claim as many as fifteen or even thirty cattle. I regret to say this law is sanctioned by the imperial government of Great Britain. Since it went into operation young men find it much easier than formerly to purchase partners for life. Avaricious old men with a plurality of wives and numerous children cannot now monopolize the wife market, continually increasing their own stock and raising the price of girls. Bartering women for cattle, as now practiced in Natal and other parts of South Africa, is not an ancestral custom of the Zulus. Fifty years ago the bridegroom presented the bride's father with three or four cows to ratify the marriage contract, and he received from the bride's relatives an equivalent in cattle or something else. Now in Natal the whole transaction previous to the celebration of the nuptials is mercenary. The natives universally admit that under British rule it has become a *bona fide* sale. Fathers call their daughters their "bank," their "stock in trade." The husband says substantially, as did Petruchio, —

"I will be master of what is my own.
She is my goods, my chattel; she is my house,
My household stuff, my field, my barn,
My horse, my ox, my ass, my anything."

None but those who have witnessed the working of polygamy in South Africa can adequately conceive the degradation and misery it involves and the strong counteracting influence it presents to philanthropic labor. Both mind and heart are brutalized by it. Should the wife be sick and unable to perform her daily task she is liable to hear from her husband the question: "Why do you not work and get back the cattle I have paid for you?" If childless, she can be returned to her home as an "unprofitable thing." If not fully paid for, her children can be taken as a mortgage till the number of cattle agreed upon is received. The Zulus are so attached to this abominable custom that nothing would so arouse their opposition to English authority as legislation which would aim at its extirpation. Not only is it idolized by the men, but, strange though it may appear, the poor degraded women who are the chief sufferers argue in favor of it. Rarely do wives object to a husband's adding to the number of helpmeets, for they say, "Now are our burdens lightened." They seemingly ignore the fact that jealousies, bickerings, and quarrels are sure to arise among a plurality of uncongenial spirits in a Zulu harem.

In intellect the women are inferior to the men, but this is doubtless attributable to the drudgery imposed upon them. To feelings of self-respect and sensitiveness under wrongs, characteristic of their more highly-favored sisters in Christian lands, they are strangers. As a rule they patiently submit to their lot, unless tortured beyond endurance by despotic husbands; but their life at the best is a hard one. The Zulu heathen wife sits in a hut of haystack architecture of one room — her parlor, kitchen, and bedroom — without window, and the door to which is two feet high; a portion of this space is fenced off for goats and calves. She prepares her husband's meal of boiled corn, ground and mixed with sour milk. He eats alone, giving what is left to the hungry children, or more hungry dogs. She must provide for herself. Fear and distrust reign there. She brings to him beer brewed from musty Indian corn, but must sip first to show that there is "no death in the pot;" while her lord and master lounges, snuffs, smokes, hunts, guzzles beer, or gads from kraal to kraal, discussing a recent case of witchcraft, or gorges himself with beef like a boa constrictor, she, with a child on her back and a heavy hoe on her shoulders, goes to the fields, digs the hard soil all day long or pulls the rank weeds from the garden, returning home at night with a bundle of firewood on her head. Not only must she serve as cart, ox, and plow, but she is expected to provide for her aged parents. Other wives come to the kraal and the strife that ensues makes her condition worse. If of a mild disposition, she tries to make the best of her lot, resigning herself meekly to her daily task. If not, she is sure to "kick against the pricks," harassing herself to no purpose. The eyes of the vigilant mother-in-law are upon her and every omission of duty is reported to her husband. No high and ennobling aspirations have a place in her soul. Her environment is one of sensuality and debasement. Death comes to her early and it is emphatically "a leap into the dark." Oh, the miseries of heathen Zulu women!

The question is sometimes addressed to missionaries from South Africa: "Are not the natives, as you find them in their free, unrestrained, normal condition, happy?" Yes, at times in a certain sense they are happy, and occasionally there gleams a ray of joy which, if developed by Christianity, would gladden their whole social life, but it is a great misnomer to call heathen joys happiness.

Inordinate beer drinking is another hindrance to the evangelization of the Zulus. Indian corn and a species of grain called amabele, after remaining in a damp place till they begin to sprout, are mashed, boiled, and then laid aside in a large dish. Yeast, obtained from an indigenous plant not unlike the ice plant, is added. When sufficiently fermented it is strained through conical bags made of rushes, into closely-woven baskets or earthen dishes. The cup for serving and drinking is made of a small gourd. The Zulus look upon their beer as food as well as drink, and often live entirely upon it. In every kraal if grain is abundant, beer is correspondingly so. From time immemorial it has been the national beverage. Where a number of kraals are located near each other, beer makers, who always are women, take turns in providing for parties of forty or fifty men, whose time is chiefly occupied in going about searching for that *sine qua non* of comfort. In winter, when women are comparatively free from hard toil, both sexes assemble almost daily for drinking and dancing. Though they do not become so thoroughly intoxicated as those who freely imbibe rum, gin, and brandy, the beer confuses their brains, rendering them foolish and often quarrelsome. A fight with knob-kerries, resulting in broken heads, is not an uncommon termination of a beer carousal. The obscenities and evil practices which accompany these orgies are so vile and harmful that from the first missionaries have felt it wise to make stringent rules for church members in regard to attending them. It was a severe trial to many to abandon a custom to which the mass of their countrymen were ardently attached, but the majority stood firm, agreeing with their instructors that spiritual loss would result if they yielded an iota. The more they were taught in respect to perils arising from social evils the stronger was their desire not only to eschew beer parties, but also feasts at which meat was sacrificed to the ancestral spirits. As a rule they acknowledged the propriety of the rules laid down by the mission churches, making it a disciplinable offense to attend such gatherings. The good effects of such rules appeared in the impetus given to the temperance cause, and after a temperance reformation in many cases there followed revivals of religion.

Another filthy and baneful Zulu practice is smoking wild hemp. This weed, easily cultivated in South Africa, abounding particularly in old deserted kraal spots, has a narcotic and even intoxicating effect, similar to that of

Indian hemp. Sometimes it is smoked in combination with tobacco, but frequently alone. The pipe used is peculiar, being the horn of an ox or large antelope with a hole about six inches from the largest end. Into this hole a reed is inserted, varying from five to eight inches in length, and where the junction is formed gum is used to render it water tight. At the upper end of the reed is attached a small soapstone bowl, in which is placed the hemp together with a live coal. The horn having been previously filled with water the smoker places his mouth at the top, inhaling with all his might the smoke that passes through the water. Having inhaled as much as he can, he closes his mouth, and with a small reed squirts the saliva upon the floor of the hut, making figures of cattle and various objects. In every kraal is found a pipe of the above description. Women do not smoke, but frequently small boys obtain access to the pipe.

Gregarious by nature, Zulus love to assemble for a grand smoke, and as the pipe is passed from one to another it is not uncommon for the smoker who has taken too much to fall on the floor full length in a state of unconsciousness. If death does not occur, his nervous system is fearfully prostrated. So injurious is this practice to body and soul that the most reliable native Christians coincide with their spiritual guides in the propriety of a church law prohibiting it on penalty of expulsion.

As obstacle after obstacle to the elevation of

the Zulus rose before us, mountain-like year after year, and we saw how inadequate were all our efforts to remove them, we were led to look away from ourselves, distrusting our own wisdom and strength, and to rely on him who has said: "Be still and know that I am God. I will be exalted among the heathen." We realized in some degree the meaning of those words: "Not by might, nor by power, but by my spirit, saith the Lord of hosts."

CHAPTER XIV.

ENCOURAGEMENTS.

LIGHT began to dissipate heathen darkness. God by visible tokens strengthened our faith. That was a joyful day in our missionary calendar on which five young men came to me and said, "We have decided to become Christians. No longer will we worship spirits or go to beer drinks. We will not become polygamists, but will live according to God's word."

More joyful still was the day when a church was organized, and we sat down for the first time with a little band of Zulu Christians to commemorate the death of our Lord. A nucleus having been formed of those on the Lord's side, some who had ridiculed our work were heard to exclaim, "We now see the power of the great King."

I was cheered concerning Dambusa, the man mentioned as lacking courage to follow the dictates of his conscience, and who appeared to be irrecoverably lost. After he had spent twelve years in a heathen kraal, in quest of a happiness which he could not find, I perceived in his countenance a restlessness that betokened a mind ill at ease. Occasionally he attended church, always taking a back seat, listening attentively to the preaching, and then retiring alone with a downcast eye. It was evident that the Holy Spirit was working in his heart. Visiting him frequently, sometimes calling him out of a noisy assembly of beer drinkers (and he never disregarded the call), taking him to some secluded place, I pressed upon him the claims of the gospel. The tears that trickled down his cheeks, with an occasional assent to my remarks, indicated deep emotion.

Dambusa had been the subject of many fervent prayers. His case had been mentioned to Christians in this country, and their petitions for his conversion were answered, though some who offered them had gone to their long home. One Sabbath, at the close of services, which had been unusually solemn, I requested him to accompany me to a cluster of trees near my house and spend a little time in religious conversation. He readily consented. In reply to the question, "How much longer are you going to resist the Spirit of God, and fight against your own conscience?" to my inexpressible joy, he said, "No longer; the controversy is ended." The penitent man poured out his soul in earnest supplication for divine help.

We trembled for him, knowing well the temptations that surrounded him. He had become entangled in the meshes of polygamy, and we were anxious to see how he would get out of them. Two or three days after, he came to us with a face radiant with joy, saying, "The way is clear. I am a free man." How he obtained his freedom, he explained. To his second married wife, for whom he had paid fifteen head of cattle, he said, "I have decided to become a Christian and live on the mission station. Will you follow my example?" Her indignant reply was, "No, not for the world, and you are a great fool!" "What will you do?" asked the husband, "for I am in earnest.' "Go home to my father's kraal and live there," answered the wife. To his first married wife he put the same question, and her reply was, "Yes, I will go with you. I have no objection to becoming a Christian." In a few weeks a neatly-built cottage appeared in front of my dwelling, into which Dambusa moved with his wife and five children. The sacrifice he made in abandoning heathenism may be seen from the fact that in giving up the second wife he also gave up her child, and the fifteen cows he had paid for her. The father of the woman not long after sold her again for ten or twelve cows, so that she was property in his hands, yielding a good investment.

I rejoice to say in regard to Dambusa that he gave great satisfaction in after years, proving a valuable helper in the work of the Lord. His regard for my wife, who taught him to read and first led him to think on religious subjects, and whom he always called "mother," was peculiarly deep and tender. He was her right-hand man in all efforts to build up the station.

Another man, who had professed to be a

Christian, but had drifted into polygamy, came to me saying that his conscience would not allow him to live in such a state. After putting away his second wife he was received into our communion. Both he and Dambusa were emphatic in their testimony that it is impossible for a man to serve God properly who has more than one wife.

When examining candidates for church membership the motives which influenced them in coming to the mission station, as they narrated them, were most interesting. I said to a young man who had decided to make a profession of his faith: "What first led you to come to us?" He surprised me by the inquiry: "Did you not call me, and have I not come? Have you forgotten that a long time ago you called one morning at a kraal, and asked a man to send his son to procure some milk for you, and that while he was milking you talked with him about the Saviour?" I replied, "I remember it perfectly." "Well," said he, "I am that boy. You called me, and haven't I come?" Joy and gratitude welled up in my heart as I realized more forcibly than ever the fulfillment of the promise, "Cast thy bread upon the waters," and I welcomed this lamb into the fold of the Good Shepherd. It was not long before heathen fathers brought their daughters to work for us, desiring payment for them. Mrs. Tyler, not having physical strength to visit the kraals, devoted her time chiefly to the training of Zulu girls who were under her eye from day to day. It taxed her patience exceedingly, but with God's help she was successful. Years after, when those whom she trained had children of their own, they brought them to their white "mother," begging her to give them the same training they had received, and saying, "We want no pay. No one can look after them like you." Feeble health prevented her from complying with many of those requests, but their appreciation of what had been done for them was a source of comfort and an illustration of the value of missionary training.

Those who attempt to Christianize barbarians discarding evangelistic methods, commit a sad mistake. It is strange that there should be any doubt on this subject after so many futile experiments. Take for instance the case of the refined, cultured, and philanthropic Bishop Colenso, who began mission work in Natal apparently under the most favorable circumstances. A large school was established, the industrial arts taught, and various branches of learning, but after a short time many of the pupils, though regarded as Christians, relapsed into heathenism. One of them, William, "the intelligent Zulu," the bishop's interpreter and principal preacher, laid aside all his civilized clothing, married four wives, and is now living in a kraal to all appearance a besotted heathen. While conversing with him a few months before I left South Africa and reminding him of his accountability to

God, he replied, with a derisive laugh, "I was taught otherwise."

I think the bishop before his death saw and sadly felt that, unless truly converted, the natives will not as a rule remain long even in a state of civilization, and yet how often the cry is echoed and reëchoed, "Civilize the Africans first, then Christianize them."

Sir Alvan Southworth, in an address before the American Geographical Society, remarked: "I have roughly computed that the Christian world has spent on missionary labor in Africa, since the era of telegraphs and railroads began, an amount sufficient to have built a railroad along the line of the equator. Let us be practical with the negro, for in his aboriginal state you cannot spiritualize him." He rejoiced that the Viceroy of Egypt was thinking of sending such missionaries as the railroad and steamboat into Central Africa. From the above, and similiar statements meeting us from all points, what are we to infer? Evidently that many who have devoted their lives to the elevation of Africa are regarded as on the wrong track, for their *modus operandi* is to preach the gospel first. But, says one, "would you preach in Africa to those dull, besotted people as you would in a civilized land?" I reply, Yes, substantially The son of Ham is yet to be found, whether Zulu or Hottentot, who cannot perceive moral distinctions — in other words, who has not a conscience, and who cannot be benefited by the simple narration of the "old, old story." If he thinks — and is there a human being incapable of thinking? — his thoughts can be directed to his Maker, his duty, and his destiny. It has been said, " As there is no philosopher too wise, so there is no child too simple, to take in God through Christ as the moral life-power in his nature." We may apply this to the lowest, most bestial tribe in heathendom. The gospel meets the deepest needs of their souls. God's spirit works through that gospel and those who proclaim it, and a change is effected without which all civilizing agencies are vain. Far be it from me to ignore the importance of civilization. It should go hand in hand with Christianity. We cannot dispense with it in elevating the degraded, but the place to which it belongs is secondary and subordinate.

In Frazer's Magazine appears a story in which a South African chief is reported to have visited England, and to have become to all appearance civilized, if not Christianized. "One day, while discoursing to a delighted audience on the importance of diffusing the blessings of civilization and the gospel, the paper collar he wore on his neck irritated him. Attempting to adjust it the buttonhole broke and he burst out with the exclamation: 'Away with this spurious civilization!' and suiting his action to his words he tore off his clothing, and stood before his audience untrammeled by civilized adornments."

I have no means of testing the truth of this

story, but it is in perfect harmony with cases which have come under my observation. The latest and most striking instance of the kind I will mention: —

About twenty-five years ago a Zulu lad, named Palma, came to me for instruction. He was uncommonly bright and inquisitive, and I had strong hopes that he would become a useful man. Tempted by some boys who ran away from their homes, he went to Durban, the seaport town of Natal, in search of work. Soon after I heard that he had gone aboard a ship bound for London, and for nearly twenty years nothing was heard from him. One day a young man with a foreign look, dressed in a sailor's suit, with a tarpaulin on his shoulder, came to my door and inquired, "Is the clergyman at home?" To my surprise it was the veritable Palma, who had returned from his wanderings. We questioned him eagerly as he related his adventures. Using the English language (for he had almost forgotten his own) he told us of his travels in Europe, Asia, and America. "How could you afford to see so much of the world?" He replied: "I have hands, and am not afraid to work." He told us of a visit he made to Dean Stanley, who asked him, "Why did you leave Africa?" His reply was, "To better my condition, sir."

As he left us for his heathen home, I cautioned him against the temptations which would assail him in his father's kraal, and he laughingly replied, "No danger." Now comes the sad part of this story. A few weeks after he reached home he doffed all his civilized clothing, and put on the skins of wild animals like his heathen relatives. He chose a wife from among the heathen, and is now living apparently with no desire for civilizing influences. His heart was not changed, alas! and he is a heathen still. Does not this story teach us that civilization alone is inadequate to elevate barbarians?

CHAPTER XV.

THE SABBATH AT ESIDUMBINI.

SOME idea of the change effected by the gospel may be formed by the description of a Sabbath at Esidumbini, a few years after the natives began to emerge from barbarism. A long loud ringing of one of Meneely's sweet-toned bells announces the return of the Sabbath. And as the sun lifts its head above the table-land in front of our dwelling, there may be seen groups of Christian Zulus wending their way to the chapel for the Sunday morning prayer meeting. The missionary's heart rejoices on seeing a goodly number assembled, for the pulse of piety on the station is determined by the interest manifested in this exercise. Wiping off the heavy dew from their bare feet they quietly seat themselves, and soon the voice of praise is heard. A sweet sound this from mouths which a short time ago were filled with obscene and senseless heathen songs. Now it is a pleasure to hear in good time, with modulated voice, and a considerable degree of taste, such tunes as Olivet, Bethany, Homer, Ariel, etc., and in words too which are full of the sweet truths of the gospel.

But listen! One of their number is leading

in prayer. That low, earnest voice is unmistakable. It proceeds from a young man who has lately given up all for Christ. The teacher steps to the veranda of his study and listens to those fervent breathings. As he confesses the black sins of years and thanks God for mercies, especially the gift of a Saviour and his precious gospel, and implores blessings on his "beloved teacher," the heart of the latter bounds with gratitude and he is nerved for the coming duties of the day.

The voice of exhortation is now heard. What says that middle-aged disciple, the teacher's right-hand man and his deacon, so long as he holds the office well? "Brothers, we are happy to-day. Our fathers died in darkness, they worshiped spirits which they believed at death enter into snakes; but we have the Bible. Brothers, what are our feelings to-day in respect to God's loving kindness to us, and our duty to him? Are we doing all in our power to make known the truth to our benighted countrymen?"

Well spoken, good fellow! I think you are sincere. You certainly did not come to the mission station for the sake of filthy lucre. Had you remained in your profession as a "medicine man," you might ere this have built for yourself a large kraal, married four or five wives, and enjoyed the world as much as any of your heathen friends; but God's Spirit reached your heart and turned the whole current of your life, and now, like

Andrew, you have found your brother Simon and brought him to Jesus.

Another voice rather plaintively breaks on the ear. Converted Zulus obey the injunction, "Confess your faults to one another." "Friends, I have done wrong. I have often heard those words of Scripture, 'Abstain from all appearance of evil;' but when I heard the singing and dancing in yonder kraal the other day, I forgot and joined the company of spectators. The teacher called me and explained the eighth chapter of 1 Corinthians, and I saw as I never did before that I was sinning against the brethren and wounding their weak consciences. I have resolved never to do this again. Pray for me." The missionary, *ex animo*: Good, there is hope for you and for the rest. The cause of God is looking up. Conscience is not asleep. God grant his aid to-day that I may speak words of encouragement to these tempted but resisting souls!

The meeting closes, and one after another thoughtfully but cheerfully retires to his home. At ten o'clock the bell announces the time for Sabbath-school. How attractive the appearance of that well-clad family, consisting of father, mother, and four daughters! They have walked a distance of eight miles, as they are accustomed to do every pleasant Sabbath, that they may receive religious instruction. There is a father bringing in his arms a little child! How unlike other Zulu men in that! The mother is delicate and inadequate to the task, but he has learned from the gospel that he should not only love his wife, but help bear her burdens. The natives take their seats and bow the head in silent prayer. The subject for the morning's sermon is the choice of Ruth, "Whither thou goest, I will go," etc., to which all heathen as well as Christians give good attention. Near the close when the question is asked, "Who among you has decided to serve God?" the missionary sees in many faces the response, "I have decided." At three P.M. the bell calls the natives to a "remembering exercise;" that is, to give account of what they recollect of the morning's discourse. Between them all the main thoughts, especially the stories, are rehearsed and then application is made of the truth to the heart and conscience. This service over, some stop to ask questions or to sing. A part of Sabbath evening the missionary has to himself, in which a sermon in English is read, then the natives of the household gather for evening prayers, and at nine o'clock all retire, none more joyful than those who can sing, "One more day's work for Jesus."

Among our children Sunday was also a day to be remembered. A friend asked my eldest daughter, not long ago, "Were Sundays made pleasant to you and your brothers and sisters when you were young and living among the Zulus?" Her reply was as follows: —

"Yes. In the first place we always had a treat of some sort for our Sunday dinner.

Nothing to make work in any way, but something we especially fancied and did not have on other days. At one time, mother had a recipe for an English bun, which she baked on Saturday for Sunday. And if we ever got leave to make sugar taffy, it was Saturday afternoon, and the candy was laid by for Sunday. Sabbath morning special books were brought out and lessons assigned to the older ones, while the little children had certain Sunday toys, not used on other days, which thus had a sort of freshness and pleasant associations. The morning service in Zulu was level to the understanding of the natives and not above that of intelligent children. We all helped in the singing, and learned to play for it after we had a melodeon. I was made a teacher of small children at seven years of age, and I had occupation for Sunday morning deciding what and how I should teach. In the afternoon we gathered round our parents, and after our lessons and little talks they showed us pictures, daguerreotypes of the friends in America, told us where they lived, and stories about them. We always walked in the garden before tea, and each was allowed to pick a bunch of flowers. Sometimes mother brought out her scrapbooks and read pieces to us, or picture books she had made, of which she was very choice, not letting us handle them ourselves. If the weather were cool, we gathered in the kitchen, and the Zulu boys and girls shared in the treat. After tea we sang with them; then father trotted the little ones on his knee, and we all went to bed early; and after mother had tucked us up we had the whispered confidences and earnest prayers that mean so much.'

CHAPTER XVI.

VISIT TO THE UNITED STATES. — NEW WORK.

TWENTY-TWO happy years rolled by, happier I think than they would have been even if I had accepted a call in 1849 from a church in Massachusetts, to become its pastor. Not a single Sabbath was I prevented by ill health from preaching. Only once was a doctor, thirty miles away, called to my house, and before his arrival the sick one was convalescent. The shield of the Almighty protected us from all harm. Twice the alarm was sounded, filling the station people with terror, "*Impi ingene!* (The enemy has come!)" but no enemy appeared. One day as I was cutting up a pig which had been killed, a letter came from the colonial office in Maritzburg, the capital of Natal, saying, "We apprehend a Zulu invasion. Flee at once to a place of safety." I said to Mrs. Tyler, who did not believe there was danger, "Shall we flee?" "Not till we have made the sausages," was her reply. The alarm was caused by a party of Zulus hunting wild pigs on the borders of the colony, and the report spread that a raid was contemplated. Had an invasion occurred, it would have been impossible for us to escape without two days' warning, as we were fifty miles from the nearest fortification, to which we should have been obliged to go in an ox-wagon. Hiding in the bush would have been our wisest course. There was an old cave a short distance from my house, once occupied by a lion, and into that we should have gone, taking food and blankets. Zulus, when on raids, do not, as a rule, spend time in " scouring the bush." What they want is cattle, and all the girls they can seize. The latter, on their return home, are distributed among them for wives.

Having charge of a printing press, from which there issued the first Zulu New Testament, two hymn books, an ecclesiastical history, and a variety of tracts, in addition to the "*Ikwezi* (Morning Star)," a monthly paper in the native language, of which I was the editor for eight years, together with preaching and itinerating among the kraals, overseeing the station, etc., the time was fully and pleasantly occupied.

While at Esidumbini the Lord gave us six children, whom we earnestly desired to see settled where they could be properly educated. This, together with a longing to meet again dear relatives, led us to ask permission to visit our native land. To part even for a season with our little church of thirty members and a body of adherents to the station, for whom we had formed a strong attachment, was a sore trial; but a native minister was appointed to take the oversight, and we broke away from them, promising to return in good time if life were spared. The two years spent in this country were intensely interesting. Visiting the churches, forming new acquaintances, the enjoyment of social, intellectual, and religious privileges, were sweet and strengthening; but all the while a feeling would come uppermost that we were needed among the Zulus and must go back as soon as practicable. Then came the great trial of our lives, with which, for depth and grievousness, none we had experienced in Africa can be compared — a trial which foreign missionaries who are parents, about to return to their fields, alone can understand — the parting with dear children. The two youngest we decided to take back with us. All we could do was to commit those left behind to the care of our covenant-keeping God.

On our return to Natal we did not renew our labors at Esidumbini. The native helper left in charge had done so well that the mission concluded to carry out a policy recommended by the Board of settling native pastors over churches established by white missionaries, thus allowing the latter to go to "regions beyond," or places where they were more needed. Our native friends and spiritual children demurred at this, calling loudly for their "father and mother"; but it seemed best to conform to the above policy. We were, however, located at Umsunduzi, a station only fifteen miles away, and were appointed superintendents of the old one. Our new home, though not so elevated and healthy as Esidumbini, was in

MISSION HOUSE AT UMSUNDUZI.

a beautiful part of the colony, twenty miles from the sea, of which it commanded a fine view. Undulating hills covered the greater part of the year with green grass and flowers, valleys and streams and numerous clusters of trees, presented a landscape never wearisome to the eye. Established by Rev. Lewis Grout in 1847, the grounds were carefully laid out and subsequently improved by Rev. William Mellen, making it exceedingly picturesque. As at all our mission stations fruit and vegetable gardens were a necessity, and we had oranges, lemons, guavas, mangoes, peaches, loquats, and pineapples. A large banana garden provided huge clusters of this delicious fruit the year round. An avenue lined by tall china trees led from the house to the chapel. At the foot of the hill on which the mission house stands is a natural fernery, in which tall trees shoot up as if trying to get beyond the ferns that twine about them. A wide field is this for biologists and botanists, so full is it of animal and vegetable life. Near the chapel is a triangular piece of ground reserved as "God's acre" with its cedar, arbor vitæ, and oleander trees, sacred to many friends.

In connection with Mr. Mellen and his family we labored till they went to America, in 1875. While together we could do more itinerating, visiting out-stations, etc. Natives willingly assembled under shady trees, or in some sheltered place, unless they had, previous to our arrival, gone to beer parties. "Kraal preaching," as we used to call this method of labor, appeared at first like "beating the air," but later experience led us to conclude that it is an important part of our work. It was "casting bread upon the waters," which was "found after many days."

Abraham, an interesting young man, trained by Mr. Mellen to evangelistic labor, asked me one Sabbath to accompany him to an out-station eight miles distant. Forty minutes' ride on horseback brought us to the end of a tableland, from which the outlook was uncommonly fine. Below us lay an immense basin filled with rivulets, and hills on which were perched numerous kraals, while near them flocks of goats and cattle were grazing. Far away to the north lay the mountains of Zululand. On the south loomed up the tabular-shaped Inanda mountain and the rugged Isangwana (Little Gate), so called from an opening on the top of a cliff. The scenery was magnificent, but alas, how devoid of anything indicating moral beauty! Like ancient Galilee, it was the "region and shadow of death." It was a relief to view in the distance one spot in which light had sprung up, Itafamasi, the station of Rev. Benjamin Hawes (a native pastor), was distinguishable six miles away by a cluster of whitewashed cottages, the abodes of Christian Zulus, and some china trees planted by Rev. Samuel Marsh, who founded the station. It was, and is now, an oasis in that moral desert.

Descending half a mile with difficulty on

account of rocks in the path, an hour's ride
through ravines brought us to the spot where
Abraham was accustomed to meet his countrymen. But to our surprise no audience appeared. Herder boys explained to us the
reason. The chief of the country had invited
his leading men to a beer drink, and they,
preferring it to the gospel, had accepted. The
Zulus not coming to us, we concluded to go to
them, and to their evident astonishment rode
into the chief's kraal and crept into the largest
hut just as the assembly were preparing for
their favorite potation. The audience that
confronted us was grotesque in the extreme.
Thirty or forty men of various ages, seated in
as small a compass as possible, destitute of
civilized clothing, their arms folded and their
chins almost resting upon their knees, occupied
every part of the hut except that devoted to
calabashes and pots of beer, and gazed on me
with curiosity. Probably they had never met
a white missionary under such circumstances.
I thought I could detect on the countenances
of a few chagrin that I should make use of
such an occasion for preaching, but the majority were apparently ready to listen and were
respectful. Zulu politeness — a natural trait —
did not forsake them, though a few were impatient. The "old, old story" was not devoid of
freshness and adaptation, though told in a Zulu
hut under seemingly adverse circumstances.
Had we been a few minutes later, drinking
would have commenced, and it would have

been difficult to get their attention. Both Abraham and myself spoke particularly of the sin of Sabbath desecration, and the chief replied: "We have done wrong! We will have no more beer parties on the day of the great King."

Mrs. Tyler, in writing to a friend in this country, about that time, observed: "We have little touches of encouragement almost every day which enable us to hold on our way with hope. This afternoon, just as I had seated myself to write to you, two heathen women came to get medicine for their children. I was glad to have an opportunity to sow a little seed in their hearts. We had a good talk about the present and the future life, and about God as *our* Father. One of them said, 'It is dreadful to think about God and to know that he is watching us all the time!' The other said she would not be sorry to die if she could see her father and be with him again. Just then my good washerwoman came with the clothes, and sat by us explaining in her own simple language what I wanted them to know. She told them that she liked to think of God as *her* Father, and added her testimony in regard to the happiness of those who are his loving and obedient children. She earnestly begged them to become the followers of Christ. The women left with subdued faces, and I hope their hearts were somewhat impressed."

Soon after she again wrote: "This morning one of my old women, who is a great comfort to me on account of the simplicity and earnestness of her faith, came for a dress to give to her little daughter that she might appear well at a wedding about to take place. At ten o'clock a small procession of girls came marching up the path leading to the chapel, escorting the bride. The bridegroom, who with his friends had been waiting some time under the shade of the trees, followed on. The ceremony over, and while the married couple were signing the marriage register, the father of the bride said he had a word of caution to give: '*You must keep your promises.* It is getting to be the custom to separate after a time, and that is worse than the heathen do, for they understand that once married there is to be no divorce!' The father previously had married all his daughters to heathen men, but he was glad to have this one united to a civilized man, though he was anxious lest she should abuse her liberty. The mother mourned over her daughters in heathenism, and this one had been of little comfort to her; but in our farewell talk I found that the bride was more tender than usual and disposed to do right. She wished to sign the temperance pledge before she went to her new home. After plenty of lemonade and a feast on bananas, all marched away, singing, to the tune of 'John Brown's body,' —

'Beer is our enemy!
Let us leave off drinking!' etc."

In another letter she said: "Last Sunday

afternoon in the service our native preacher conducted, he spoke on the subject of genuine conversions, and alluded particularly to Silas Nembula, with whom he attended school at Adams: 'The brightest scholar, the one to whom we all resorted for help in translating into English, in arithmetic or anything we required — but he was a boy like ourselves. When he gave himself to Christ we did not need to ask if he were a true Christian; he was so humble no one doubted it. All knew that he had learned of the Master that beautiful Christian humility which he maintained till his death.'"

Silas was the grandchild of Monasi, the first convert to Christianity among the Zulus.

CHAPTER XVII.

EXPERIENCES AT UMSUNDUZI.

IT took us some time to become acquainted with the kraals occupying the mission reserve of about six thousand acres at Umsunduzi, but after that everything went smoothly. The heathen were friendly and our Sabbath congregations large and attentive. To show that an African missionary's life is not a monotonous one, I give the experience of one day.

At sunrise a rap on our front door announced the arrival of the postman, who was to take our letters to Verulam, the nearest European village, a distance of fifteen miles. Rising hurriedly I tied up the postal matter, put it in a bag made of wagon canvas, gave the carrier sixpence with which to purchase his dinner, and a caution not to waste his time and mine snuffing by the way. While at breakfast word came that Jack, the horse I was intending to ride while visiting the people, had a swollen leg. A bottle of "imbrocation" was given to the horse-boy, with directions how to use it, and I returned to my morning meal. During family prayers in English, natives were assembling in the yard in front of the house, each on important business. One mother took down from a leather shawl tied pouch-like on her back a child of six months who had caused her sleepless nights. A dose of castor oil with two of santonine, and explanations how to administer the latter, and the woman left with a lighter heart. Another said that her baby had crept into the fire during the night and was badly burned. A little Turner's cerate, with a cloth for bandage, etc., and this sad mother departed. The next patient was a tall, athletic man, who did not appear ill in the least. But he insisted that bile was killing him, and nothing would satisfy him but a big dose of jalap and calomel. While carefully measuring the latter, he said, "Put in more; black people need twice as much as you whites." This man attended to, another appeared with a long face and a piteous story. He had incurred a debt, and inquired if I could not lend him twenty-five dollars for a few months. Without stopping to give a lecture on the importance of keeping free from debt, but saying, "You know well that we missionaries are not money-lenders," I dismissed this last of my morning callers.

Mounting my horse I proceeded to a kraal about a mile from my house. The headman I found seated outside the door of one of the huts chatting earnestly with some of his neighbors. After a polite salutation, for Zulu men usually observe their rules of etiquette, I was invited to sit by his side on a wooden stool, which is also used as a pillow. The matter under discussion was of deep interest. It seemed that a certain woman had been seriously ill, but her illness was of a peculiar nature. She was possessed with evil spirits, and all efforts on the part of her friends to exorcise these spirits had been unsuccessful. "But," said I, "this must be stopped. I cannot allow her to live on the mission reserve if she practices arts of divination, which she is evidently wishing to do." "Alas! teacher, we know it," said they, "but how to stop it we cannot tell. It is beyond our power." Promising to see the woman myself and use my influence to change her designs, and invoking the aid of almighty God in turning from darkness to light not only this unfortunate individual but all the victims of superstition, I went to another kraal.

This had but two huts in it, and its owner was a young man, the possessor of two wives. There was an appearance of poverty about the place. The cattle fold held no cows. I asked the usual question, "Are you well?" "No; I am not well;" and his next sentence explained the cause. "We have famine here." "Where are your cattle?" "Gone to pay for my second wife," was the response. "Ah, I see the cause of your trouble. But you have only yourself to blame. You have been told many times that polygamy is not a custom pleasing to our Master, the Lord Jesus Christ; and you knew better than to part with all your cows to gratify your vile passions." "Oh, this is the custom of black people! We cannot abandon it," was his reply.

After a few words of admonition and entreaty I rode to another Zulu dwelling — an upright house neatly thatched and whitewashed. Outside, the grounds were tidy and the inside was no less so. Seated in an American chair, I had a pleasant chat with the occupants. I had come into quite a different atmosphere — into a Christian home. Various plans were discussed for bringing the heathen people about us to feel their need of the gospel and to send their children to the station school. Prayer was offered, in which all joined with reverence. Then I returned home.

Dinner over, there were a dozen or more little matters to be attended to, letters to write, native boys to have work given them, and then came the weekly temperance meeting conducted by my native assistant. All were urged most earnestly to refrain from all kinds of evil, drinking beer especially. Then a discussion ensued which was not ended till sundown, and one young man had signed the pledge. Before tea several attendants at meeting requested an interview, and then we sat down to our evening meal. Soon the postman arrived, and for a short time we were in a state of excitement hoping to see some American letters and hear of our dear ones over the sea. We were, however, disappointed. The bell for evening prayers was rung, after which four boys and three girls were instructed, and then came a time of quiet and freedom before retiring.

About the same time Mrs. Tyler recorded as follows a day of *her* experience : —

"Awakened by the sound of horse's hoofs on the hard walk in front of the house, I found it was the traveler who had spent the Sabbath with us, starting for home. Breakfast on hasty pudding as usual, with syrup, as our milk did not reach us in time. When the school-teacher came, he told me what some of the people had said at the prayer meeting on the preceding day. One of the church members had broken his pledge and drunk beer at different places, for which he was very sorry, and wanted all to pray for him that he might try again.

"Another said he saw more and more that it was better to have nothing to do with beer in their houses, and, although he had not signed the pledge, nor taken the 'blue ribbon,' he had taken none for a long time. Moreover, when invited by his married son to go to his house and partake of a feast where there was beer, he had declined, saying that 'the presence of beer would spoil all that was rational.'

"The school bell rang, the native girls hastened to their studies, and I was left alone for quiet reading, as I hoped. The Gospel of John is now our study in Sunday-school, and we naturally turn to it for private reading, so as to gather up and have ready all we can for our classes. Last Sunday one of the men remarked that he had read Mary's words to the servants in the second chapter, fifth verse: 'Whatsoever he saith unto you, do it'; but it never occurred to him how it could be applied to us. 'So it is,' he added, 'we are all the time finding something new in the Bible.' While I was reading, there was a knock, and an old church member with his wife came for a little talk. In the midst of our conversation a fine-looking heathen man appeared, in search of medicine for his child, who had rolled into the hot ashes at night and burned the whole side of one leg. He joined so intelligently in our conversation, I was led to inquire where he learned so much. He said he had lived with several missionaries, giving their names, and knew all about the Bible and our religion. When I asked if it were not worthy of reception, he replied, 'Yes; it is good and right; but when I saw how many promised to be Christians and then broke their promises, I said it was worse than not to make any. So I am trying to be good *without* promises.' This is the excuse of many who have been taught in our mission stations, as we know it is in Christian lands. Individual responsibility seems to have little meaning to these people. It is not uncommon to hear them say, 'We are content to die and go where our fathers are.'

"The next call was from a young man who came to borrow money of my cook, to pay his subscription to the home mission fund. After much talk between them, and a promise that it should be returned in two months, he took the money and departed. I felt bound to give him a short lecture on industry, as I had noticed him the week previous going about among his friends to visit and talk, instead of working to earn the money he needed.

"The afternoon came, and the bell rang for the usual prayer meeting. Soon there appeared my good old washerwoman asking for the money she had earned and left with me, in order that she might put it into the treasury of the 'Home Missionary Society.' Every year she pays her subscription of $1.25. This year wages are low, and the people find it difficult to get clothing and other requisites; so we are not surprised to find their contributions less than usual. After the meeting in which the claims of home missions were discussed and subscriptions received, I found among the names of contributors one who had put down a *goat*. I asked him how he would carry it to the meeting which was at hand. He smiled, saying he had engaged a friend to sell it for him, so that he might carry the money. He did not reflect he might have done this a month ago, and thus be sure of the money in time, but waited until the last moment before saying anything about it. This is characteristic of the Zulus. One of our old missionaries has truly said: 'We do not need to preach to the Zulus on the text, Take no thought for the morrow. They obey that literally.'

"Tea over, the native boys belonging to our household came in to read, and we had a pleasant talk on the chapter that was read, till eight o'clock, when I dismissed them and called in our two little kitchen girls, to look after their clothing. One of them was full of smiles when she found that I had a nice dress that would fit her, and gave me a hearty 'Thank you.' I suppose she never had but one dress before at a time, and when that was washed was obliged to wrap herself in a shawl or old garment of her mother's. The girls retired happy, and I had an hour for sewing and thinking in perfect quiet. My mind wandered back to our first days in Africa and along down to the present time. Days of joy and sadness, of happiness and trial, of success and disappointment, loomed up before me; and I saw so much of the kindness and goodness of our heavenly Father to us that at the close I could almost forget everything else; and I hastened to retire that nothing might come between me and the sweet peace that seemed to come so directly from above."

The mission has not seen fit to locate a white missionary at Umsunduzi since ill health obliged me to resign my charge of the station. But the people are fortunate in having as acting pastor a native whose name is a peculiar one — Bontyise, which is the Zulu for *beans*. Zulus, like the Jews, are in the habit of naming their children after some circumstance connected with their birth; and that vegetable was introduced into the locality of his birth at the time he was born. Bontyise was given to me by his father, who was dying of consumption in a heathen kraal. I said to him, "That little boy will soon be without a father. Give him to me, and I will be a father to him." The wives, of whom there were six, all heard him give his assent, and after his father's decease the lad came to me. I had him educated at Adams, under the Rev. William Ireland, and on my return to Natal, after my first visit to the United States, Bontyise came to me that he might study, preparatory to preaching the gospel. While pursuing his studies, he taught the daily school at Umsunduzi, and on my leaving South Africa assumed the charge of the station. The last letter I received from him manifests his feelings, which I doubt not are genuine: —

My dear Father, — I regret to learn that you do not feel able to return to us. I hoped to see you again in the flesh; but if, in the course of divine providence, I never shall, and if I should be called to die first, then I will ask my heavenly Father to allow me to sit at one of the windows of heaven and keep on the lookout for you; and when you come, I will say to him: "There is my beloved teacher"; and there will be no more any sea to separate us. We shall be forever with the Lord.

CHAPTER XVIII.

ZULU CHURCHES.

IN the first days of our mission Zulu marriages were not legal in the eyes of the Natal authorities unless cattle were paid; but this has been remedied, and mainly through the intervention of missionaries. At present if the father or brother of the girl to be married states to the English magistrate, before witnesses, that he will not call for cattle, it is recorded, and the marriage is legal. Another step in advance has been taken. If a man is married according to Christian rites, and takes another wife, he is liable to be punished for bigamy. To such a degree does the custom of *ukulobola* feed the avarice of the father and foster indolence on the part of the brothers, to say nothing of its degrading effect on the home life, that missionaries of various bodies in Natal have considered it wise to make it a church disciplinable offense, the Americans taking the lead.

In 1879, after careful discussion with native pastors and lay helpers, a set of regulations for the churches under our supervision was adopted. They ruled out polygamy, barter in women, beer-drinking parties, all intoxicating drinks, and the smoking of wild hemp.

Frequent cases of discipline — especially for barter in women — occurred; but natives on whose judgment we could rely often assured us that the rules were none too strict. It was gratifying to see that some church members legislated concerning these customs without suggestion from their white teachers.

A church organized with fifteen members under Nqumba, a native pastor at Imputyane, near Adams, has the following laws, made and adopted by themselves: —

I. No polygamist shall be allowed to become a member of this church.

II. He who sells his daughter or sister treats her like a horse or cow, and cannot be received into this church.

III. The man who has lost his wife is not allowed to live with another woman unless they are married, and a widow is not allowed to live with a man unless they are married.

IV. No young man or woman shall be allowed to marry according to heathen customs.

V. No member of this church shall be permitted to attend a wedding if beer is drunk there, although he may have been invited to it.

VI. No member of this church shall be permitted to drink the "white man's grog," or native beer, nor touch it with his lips.

VII. No beer shall be made on this station, and all who come here from other stations must conform to this rule.

VIII. No member of this church is allowed to smoke wild hemp or tobacco. They take away reason, knowledge, and good character.

IX. No member of this church is allowed to go where there is slaughtering for the departed spirits. Those who have fellowship with those who do so slaughter countenance this superstition and are not worthy of church fellowship.

Polygamous converts would occasionally apply for admission into the church, and in cases where there seemed to be religious sincerity and earnestness it was hard to shut the door against them. A striking case occurred at Umsunduzi. A man of considerable intelligence and reputed good character came to me with his two wives, each of whom had four children, and asked permission to build on the mission reserve, saying, "I have heard of the Christian religion, and I wish to know more about it." No more eager listener to the Word ever came within sound of my voice, and the conversations we had with him revealed very clearly that he was determined to find out the truth. He set about learning to read, and within ten months could read in the New Testament. In respect to the domestic entanglement into which he had entered before he came to the station and previous to his knowledge of Christianity, I instructed and advised him to the best of my ability. He professed to see, and I believe did see, that polygamy is an evil and not in accordance with the teachings of the gospel, but how to get out of it was the question. He said to me with deep emotion, "I have decided to serve God, and wish to obey him in all things." I told him to look upward and pray fervently for the guidance of the Holy Spirit, assuring him that, if he did so, he would receive divine direction. He promised to do this. Soon after he rehearsed to me the difficulties under which he labored. He said to his second wife, "Will you leave me? You see the fix I am in. God's Word does not sanction polygamy. As I am now I cannot connect myself with the people of God." She replied, "You are my husband. I cannot love another man. I also want to be a Christian. Besides, there are the children. Who will look after their best interests as well as their father? No; I cannot leave you. Where thou goest I will go;" etc. A similar response came from his first married wife. It is no wonder that both chose to stick to him, for he is the most amiable Zulu husband I ever knew.

Baffled in this attempt to extricate himself, he concluded to let the matter alone for a while, but to do his duty as a Christian. All his children were placed under instruction, the eldest son being sent to Lovedale College in Kaffraria, where he stayed seven years and shone brilliantly as a scholar; another son became a teacher at Adams, and several of the daughters completed a course of education at Lindley. The father has grown in Bible knowledge and stability of Christian character. Both of the wives have also manifested a desire to join the church. The question arises, What are we to do with such cases? Some might say, as was said to me more times than one, "Admit them into the church; you have no right to refuse." It is easy to give advice, but, viewing the matter in all its lights, I am convinced it is not proper to receive polygamous converts to church fellowship. I agree with what Rev. John Paton, that most heroic missionary of modern times, has said of the natives at Aniwa (an island of the New Hebrides) when placed in similar circumstances:— "How could we have led natives to see the difference betwixt admitting a man to the church who had two wives and not permitting a member of the church to take two wives after his admission? Their moral sense is blunted enough without knocking their heads against a conundrum in ethics. In our church membership we have to draw the lines as sharply as God's Word will allow, betwixt what is heathen and what is Christian, instead of minimizing the difference."

CHAPTER XIX.

ZULU CHRISTIANS.

TO abandon heathenism and live a consistent Christian life requires, on the part of Zulus, considerable moral courage. Their piety is sometimes severely tested. We had at Umsunduzi a woman whose husband was for years a son of Belial, persecuting his wife fearfully whenever she manifested a desire to serve God. Her trouble began while we were at Esidumbini, to which station she once fled, hoping that we should be able to protect her. So long as she remained in our house, we could do so, for a white man's house in Natal is his castle, into which no native dares enter without permission; but the cunning husband, who was on the watch, caught her one day outside, seized her by the arm, and dragged her away. We had advised her to bear meekly the treatment she received and to pray earnestly that God would soften her husband's heart. Faku — for that was his name — after a while ceased annoying her, and even allowed her to attend church. She saw that her prayers were being answered. Great was her joy when she perceived a willingness on his part to move his residence to the mission station that the children might attend the daily school. She had been in the habit of gathering them together for family prayer, and when he was present she saw that he was interested. She ventured to ask him to pray. At first he declined, but afterwards would occasionally take her place, and she noticed a gradual softening in his speech and behavior. This led her to pray more fervently. One Friday afternoon at the usual prayer meeting when opportunity was given for any one to speak, Faku rose and in a very humble way told his experience: how he knew he had been sinning against light, that his heart had been bound by Satan, and that it seemed as if he never could free himself from his grasp. But now he trusted he had found help in Christ and that he should never stray from him. He said he had sold all his older daughters for cattle, but not a cow was to be seen in his cattle fold. Like other earthly treasures, they were all swept away, and he wanted to feel that in Christ he had found a treasure he should never lose. He had been cruel to his wife; but she had always been good to him and unwearied in her efforts to lead him in the right way. All who heard him felt that he was saved in answer to *her prayers*. Her face wore a look of glad surprise. No one spoke for a few minutes, when she, in a quiet tone, observed: "We see how God loves us; we do not know how to love him as we ought." Then she knelt and thanked God for his unspeakable love. One of the native church members of long standing, who heard her pray, said he never saw such humility. It made him feel that he was far below her in Christian attainment. Amid all the troubles that good woman experienced, her hope and comfort were in prayer. She expected God to answer her petitions, although she might have to wait many days before the answer came.

Instances occurred in which men living in their native kraals were impressed by the truth and commenced a new life without going to the station and living in houses built in European style, as the majority of converts were in the habit of doing. A tall man, clad in the ordinary attire of the skins of wild animals, was seen in our chapel one Sabbath, with a countenance indicative of deep interest. Unlike most of the men he took his seat in the Sabbath-school. Mrs. Tyler, who was always on the lookout for opportunities to deepen any impression the truth may have made, found that he was under conviction of sin and anxious to know the way of salvation. It was not long before he became a decided Christian, and then he endeavored to bring his wife and two children to the sanctuary. Frequent interviews with him convinced me that he was a humble and sincere believer. But he lived only a few months after his conversion. Word reaching me that he was ill, I went to him at once, taking such medicines as I thought he required. I found him seated on the ground outside of his hut apparently in great pain. Thanking me for the medicine, he remarked, to my surprise, "I shall be no better; the Lord is calling me to himself." He then spoke of his gratitude for all I had done for him, particularly for my instruction, and said, "I ask you to be a father to my two children, who will soon have no earthly father to look after them. . . . I am not afraid to die. I shall soon be with Jesus, and I expect to meet you in the heavenly world." After a little conversation and prayer I told him that I hoped the medicine would relieve him, for I did not consider his illness of so serious a nature.

Before leaving, I noticed a freshly dug hole about three yards from the place where the sick man was seated, and wondered what it was for, but made no remarks. The next day tidings came that he died at early dawn; and before I could reach the kraal his two little ones, a girl of twelve years and a boy of ten, had dragged the body to that freshly dug hole which I had noticed the preceding day, and there they buried it. The mother, ill at the time, was so weakened by the shock that she could render the children no assistance. The latter, when asked why they did not apply to their neighbors for help in burying their father, replied that the native custom was to pay a cow and calf and a goat for "the washing of the hands," which they were too poor to give.

I took the boy to my home and placed him in school, leaving the girl with the mother.

When I went after her a few months later, a heathen relative had claimed her as his property and refused to give her up. Illustrations of the power of the gospel to sustain and comfort in a dying hour I have seen among the Zulu people, but none where the environment was one of such deep poverty as in the case just described.

Another kraal man was awakened from his heathen slumber on a Sabbath day. He was rich in cattle and was contemplating the purchase of a second wife. The state of his lungs prevented his coming to the station for instruction, so I visited him frequently, holding religious services in his hut. For several weeks he was under conviction, and when he indulged a hope of pardon his joy and peace were indescribable. All his heathen neighbors marked the change. As he desired to join the company of Christ's followers and make a public confession of his faith, I went to his kraal one Sabbath afternoon, taking with me one of my daughters and twenty members of the Umsunduzi church. About the same number of heathen men and women joined us, filling the hut to overflowing. After a brief service, followed by baptism and the Lord's Supper, I gave the sick man an opportunity to make a few remarks. He took a passage of Scripture he had heard me comment upon: "I am the way, the truth, and the life." I will translate literally his words on the first part of that passage : —

"My friends, you see that I am soon to die, but I have no fear. Jesus is my Saviour, and he will support me. He is the way. There is no other way. I have tried the ways of the world in search of peace and happiness, but all in vain till I found the Lord Jesus. My last words to you, my friends, are, 'Make the Saviour *your* friend.' He will not only pardon your sins, but will comfort you when you are about to leave the world, as he is now comforting me."

An unusual solemnity was apparent on the countenances of his heathen relatives, as one after the other they crept out of the hut and went quietly to their homes. The man died soon after in the triumphs of faith.

A Christian Zulu father, in writing about the death of his son, whose name was Ukani, said: "You would like to hear some of his last words. He said to me: 'Do you know that death has overcome me? Please call all the children of our house.' They came. He looked upon them and wept. He remarked: 'I do not cry because of fear of death, but because you have not become Christians.' He talked to them a short time on religious subjects, and then said: 'I do not know whether the morning will find me here.' He wanted me to read to him from Bunyan's Pilgrim's Progress — a book of which he was very fond — and the fourteenth and fifteenth chapters of John's Gospel. He rejoiced very much when prayer was offered. When I asked him what I should pray for, he replied: 'That I may be strengthened in the Lord.' Once he prayed that the Lord would come and take him out of the world, and said: 'Father, the Lord does not hear me.' I trembled, and said: 'Why not?' He replied: 'Because death does not come.' He then added: 'I do not complain. It is the Lord's will that I endure the pain. His will be done.'

"I cannot write all the 'little crumbs' of his talk. On Thursday he said to his mother: 'I see a little of the place to which I am going. I see a beautiful city, and this side of it a river. The city has many people in it, and it is very nice.' On Friday he said to me: 'Father, do not sleep to-night, for I feel that death has taken fast hold of me.' At four o'clock he called for his mother, but before she arrived he leaned his head back and died. His face was as if he were sleeping."

A Christian Zulu woman died at the Umvoti station in the enjoyment of perfect peace. One who was an eyewitness reported her as saying, "I know that I am dying, but why should I fear to go home? I love my Saviour. I love my God. I have no fear. All is so bright." Her last words were: "Jesus, my Saviour!"

A married man by the name of Kalo, on the same station, when about to expire, said to his weeping friends: "I so greatly rejoice to go to Jesus in heaven! I feel I am in the right way. Love him, all of you! Wife, cling to your faith; teach the children, keep them as Christians should be. Let us all meet in heaven!"

It would be easy to present more illustrations of the power of Christianity to comfort the soul in a dying hour, which have come under my observation during the period of my missionary labor among the Zulus. The above must suffice. The gospel, and that alone, can impart peace to the converted African when crossing the "dark river," as it does to Christians of other countries and other climes.

A ZULU PREACHER AND FAMILY.

CHAPTER XX.

ZULU PREACHERS.

IT was a prediction of President Edwards that "the Ethiopian might in time become very knowing in divine things." There are no instances in which educated Zulus have attained to distinction in divine knowledge, but that some have so studied the Bible and had their hearts so permeated by the Holy Spirit that they have been truly eloquent, I can testify from personal observation. For direct, earnest appeal to the conscience I have never seen them surpassed. They do not always adhere to their texts; but they have this sterling characteristic, which cannot be said of all ministers at the present day in their preaching: as the late Robert Moffat has told us of the Bechuana preachers, "they are careful never to go out from between Genesis and Revelation."

No attempt to frighten a Zulu preacher has as yet been successful. A Trappist monk said to one, "You must stop preaching." The native, who was holding a padlock in his hand at the time, replied, "If you should fasten my mouth with this lock, and go away with the key, I would not cease to proclaim the gospel."

Seven Zulu ministers have received ordination at the hands of American missionaries. The majority have done well. Three have gone to their reward.

Rev. James Dube was pastor of the church at Lindley, the station named after its beloved founder. When a youth like other Zulu lads, Dube was assailed by temptations, but in his case there was special danger, for he was the son of a chief, and a large and influential tribe looked to him as their future ruler. The emoluments of Zulu chieftainship are great and exceedingly fascinating in the eyes of the natives. Dube knew well that if he remained in heathenism he would inherit, not only power, but wealth, consisting of cattle, by which he could purchase as many wives as he desired. In the providence of God he was brought under the influence of Mr. and Mrs. Lindley, who were quick to see the danger to which he was exposed, and the good of which he might be instrumental if he became a Christian. By wisdom and kindness they won him to the mission station and urged on his attention the claims of the gospel. To their joy his heart responded favorably. He agreed to abandon spirit worship and to give up all thought of becoming a polygamist. His teachers prayed most earnestly with him and for him, nor did they pray in vain. For some time Dube was under deep conviction. He experienced thoroughly what divines in New England, near the beginning of the century, called "law work." When he decided to serve

REV. JAMES DUBE.

God, it was no halfway decision. A more complete transformation of character among the Zulus I never knew. He encountered opposition, and at that period of our mission's history it was bitter and determined. Satan tried all his arts to persuade him to return to his heathen kraal and the vile customs of his people. All the "glories" of heathenism were set before him, but in vain. His thirst for knowledge, especially that of the Bible, was intense, and it was a real joy to guide his inquiring mind in the study of the Holy Scriptures. For a year or more he studied under Rev. David Rood. He then taught school, but before Mr. Lindley left Natal the last time, Dube was unanimously invited to the pastorate of the church of which he was a member. The ordination scene was one I shall never forget. The charge to the pastor was given by Mr. Lindley, Dube's spiritual father; and with tears rolling down his cheeks the venerable missionary remarked: "This is the gladdest day of my life. I never anticipated beholding such a sight as this."

From the time Mr. Dube assumed the oversight of the Lindley church till his death he labored with zeal and fidelity. That love of money was not one of his besetting sins is evident from the fact that for years he did not take a farthing for his services, saying, "My people are poor, and I can support myself." Mrs. Edwards, who has charge of the High School for Girls at Lindley, could always rely on his help when needed. His love for all Christian missionaries, especially those to whom under God he attributed his conversion, was marked and constant. In common with his friends, who said that if their "father and mother" (Mr. and Mrs. Lindley) must leave them to die and be buried in another land, the expense of their burial should come upon their children, he contributed liberally towards the fund of one hundred dollars which was sent to America to be held in trust for that object. As a preacher he was earnest and persuasive. His imposing personal appearance was in his favor. Over six feet in height, with a body symmetrically proportioned, a penetrating eye, and a voice easily heard in the largest church, he always made a deep impression on his hearers.

I once heard an English missionary from Kaffraria observe, while dilating on the eloquence of a native preacher, "For that man's talent in pulpit oratory I would willingly give my right arm." I never arrived at that pitch of enthusiasm while listening to Zulu ministers, but I often wished that the Lord would enable me to proclaim the truth as eloquently as did James Dube.

The death of this interesting man was sudden. One of his last utterances was, "Christ to me is precious." When it was announced to the people of his tribe that he was dead, their grief was profound and protracted. Week after week natives were seen wending their way, some of them from a long distance, to the grave to shed tears of sorrow and condole with the bereaved family. All the members of our mission felt that we had sustained an irreparable loss.

Another Zulu pastor, also deceased, was Rev. Ira Adams, named thus after a brother of his teacher, Rev. Newton Adams. His mother, Umbulazi, was the first convert to Christianity among the Zulus. Living in the family of the missionary for ten years or more, Ira had an opportunity to acquire the English language, which he spoke with ease and fluency. For a time he engaged in the sugar enterprise and became in part owner of a mill. To an officer of the Natal government who congratulated him once on his success, he said, " Yes; it is all the result of missionary instruction." While employed in secular pursuits he preached among the kraals every Sabbath. Elected to the pastorate of the church at Adams, he labored a few years, but ill health obliged him to move to another part of the colony, where he died deeply regretted.

The third Zulu pastor, also deceased, was Rev. Umsingapansi, a man of sterling worth, who was converted through the instrumentality of Rev. James Bryant. Preaching, or, as he expressed it, " taking up the cause of God that lay on the ground," during the temporary absence of Rev. William Ireland, Mr. Bryant's successor, he continued his ministrations till called unanimously to the oversight of the

Ifumi church. His death, after six years of faithful labor, was a sore bereavement. Two of the four surviving pastors have not proved a comfort and joy to those who inducted them into the sacred office. One, engaged in trading, became involved in debt, left his people, and took up his abode in the Zulu country. Another, for immorality and apparent untruthfulness, was suspended from the ministry, but is now living a Christian life.

These defections have led missionaries to be cautious in ordaining Zulu preachers. Though they can talk eloquently and pray as if inspired from above, they do not all possess that *moral backbone* which is desirable. These cases of lapse, as can be easily imagined, furnished material for skepticism in regard to the results of missions. "See," said some, "how badly that native preacher has turned out!" Missionaries, of course, had to come in for a share of blame. One black sheep attracted more attention than fifty good ones. They seemed to ignore the fact that in civilized lands cases often occur in which persons who have stood high in church and society have committed flagrant offenses, while no one thought of blaming the clergymen whose ministry they attended.

A few specimens of addresses on different occasions will show the character of the native preaching.

In 1873, when Mr. and Mrs. Lindley were about to leave South Africa, after thirty-eight

Zulu Evangelist, Wife, and Child.

years of faithful labor, there was a gathering of Zulu converts, at which one of them spoke as follows: —

"Brothers and sisters, we can but weep, for to-day we are but orphans. Our father and mother are now dead to us. Our hearts are all too full of grief for many words. Who will wipe away our tears now? Who will toil for us as patiently and bear with us in love as they did? . . . Their leaving is caused only by the sickness of our mother. She can work for us no longer; she has worked too hard. Others will be kind to them and take care of them, but they will not find any children to love them better than we do. . . .

"Let us review the past a little; it will do us good. Turn to the old deserted home under the Inanda Mountain. There is no spot to us on earth like that. There we were boys, when our father came with his wagon and commenced building his house. There we saw one and then another believing and building on the station. There we were taught and felt our hearts growing warm with love to God and to his Son. A few weeks ago I rode past that loved and beautiful place. My heart was full of old memories. I saw the bush where we went and made our first prayer. We hardly knew what made us pray. We were naked, ignorant herder boys. I said, 'Who is this now riding on a good horse, with a saddle and bridle? He is well dressed, so that this cold wind is not felt. Verily, it is the same herder boy! What a contrast! And where is he going? To see his children, who are in two large boarding schools, one at Amanzimtote, the other here at Inanda.' Did we in those days, when we knew not how to hold a book,— knew not which side was up or which was down,—think it would be all like this to-day? No; really, no. Goodness and mercy have followed us. See how we have increased! Look into our houses; see what comforts! Our cup is running over. . . .

"We must now put on the armor and work more earnestly, for we have to take up our father's work. May his mantle fall on us! and may we salt our work as he salted his by a blameless example! . . .

"We have come to hear our father's last words, and to bury him. So we will send the money over the sea, that others may not bury him. This is the only way that we can show that we are his children. Let us henceforth live in peace and love as children in one family should do. It will then prove that our father and mother did not spend their lives in useless work. Above all, let us earnestly pray that we may have this gathering together once more, but not on earth. We want it to be in heaven. There our tears will all be wiped away."

Another, while discoursing on the Bible, said:—

"Wise men have made a telescope by which they can see other suns and other moons and other stars — many more than we can see with our eyes. But the greatest telescope is the Book made by God. It brings God's character to our view. We can see his holiness and benevolence. It brings Christ to our view. We hear his words; he walks and talks with us. It is a wonderful telescope because it draws us to him and binds us to him forever. It shows us the way to heaven; we see its beauty and brightness and joy. We see also those great, strong believers — old Abraham, Isaac, and Jacob, who had faith to believe what we call improbabilities."

Said another, making use of imagery familiar to his hearers: —

"The gospel is a great wagon laden with salvation. Christ told his disciples that it is to be carried to all nations. Believers are Christ's oxen — the load is to go and be distributed among all the inhabitants of the world. If the oxen are lazy, God will take them out and put others in, those that will draw. Who of us are drawing the gospel wagon? If we are not, we shall find ourselves left out, and others will be put in our place. Turn not away because the wagon is heavy. Pull, and strength will be given to you."

Still another: —

"What would you think if you should come into a house and see a man lying on his mat, looking ill, and you should ask, 'What is the matter?' and he replied, 'Nothing at all'? You say, 'Tell me, that I may help you. Where is your pain?' 'I tell you, I am quite well,' replies the man. You beg him to allow you to send for the doctor, but he refuses. Just so it is with sinners. You see that they are ill, and wish them to send for the Great Physician, but they do not see it. What shall we think of them?"

CHAPTER XXI.

ZULU CUSTOMS AND LAWS.

THE various tribes in South Africa are popularly called *Kaffirs*. Arab traders, who were Mohammedans, gave them this name, which signifies *infidels*, or those who would not embrace their faith. The term "Zulu Kaffirs" is often used to distinguish the Amazulu from other tribes, or what has been called the Bantu race. This word Bantu, as Mr. Stanley remarks, is unphilosophical and perfectly meaningless, as it signifies merely men, or people. The Zulus, being a distinct nation, should go by the name of Zulus, and by no other.

Their ethnology does not furnish data sufficient to allow us to speak with certainty as to their origin. That they differ from the Demarara and other tribes in Southwestern Africa, and from the Hottentots near the Cape of Good Hope, we have abundant proof. With the latter there is not the least natural affinity, although a few Hottentot *clicks* appear in the Zulu as well as in some other South African languages.

A tribe of cannibals called Amazitu, living on Lake Tanganyika, from the description given by explorers, appear to be pure Zulus. Their dialect is the same that is spoken in

Zululand. Mr. Stanley's "In Darkest Africa" speaks of being "in the presence of twin brothers of Zululand, tall, warlike creatures with Caucasian heads and faces," in a district called Uhha, but he does not tell us what language they speak.[1] In the vocabularies of Schweinfurth, Cameron, and other travelers, unmistakable Zulu words appear, which tend to show that the maritime Zulus in the south, and other tribes at the north, may have had a common origin, but where their primeval home was we cannot tell. Some of their customs are quite Jewish; as, for instance, the practice of circumcision, and, till a late date, rejection of swine's flesh; the fear to step on a newly-made grave lest they contract a disease of the feet; the custom of widows marrying the brothers of their former husbands; the naming of children after some circumstance connected with their birth; their sacrifical offerings; the observance of the feast of firstfruits; the purchase of wives; the ceremony of attaching to a cock the diseases of

[1] In a recent interview between Rev. George Wilder, missionary to the Zulus, and Mr. Stanley, the latter related that he had in his party a Zulu woman from Natal who was able to converse with the Wahuma, a tribe living near the Mountains of the Moon. They said: "This woman is one of our people; where did she come from?" Not only in language, but in customs, those people resemble the Zulus. The Abangoni, living on Lake Nyasa, are also Zulus. The Zulu dialect is the court language of Manica country, under the chief Ungungunhama, son of Umzila. This is the auriferous region which has been under dispute between the Portuguese and the British South Africa Company. The Matabele are, it is well known, pure Zulus. There is an evident kinship between tribes living all the way along from Natal to Albert Nyanza, so that one understanding thoroughly the Zulu tongue has a key by which to unlock the various dialects spoken in Eastern Africa.

the people, and sending it by a fit person into the wilderness, like the Jewish scapegoat; the punishment of the slayer of a king with death; the cursing of an enemy before going to war; the custom in the kraals of having water poured on their hands after a meal by servants; the eating with a spoon from one dish; the sprinkling of the doorway of a hut with medicinal water to keep away disease; the piling up of memorial stones, etc.

They have also traditions of events that happened in the earliest days of which we have record, and Zulu Christians often exclaim, "We understand the Old Testament better than the New; it describes so perfectly our home life!"

There are some who locate the Ophir [1] of the Bible in Southeastern Africa, maintaining that certain ruins discovered by Mauch, the German traveler, in latitude 20°, not far from Port Sofala, are the veritable "Solomon's mines." But thus far no satisfactory proof has been adduced that they are anything more than the ruins of old Portuguese forts.

The number of aboriginal Zulus in Natal is

[1] An English archæologist has lately gone to Mashonaland for the purpose of removing the *débris* that has accumulated for centuries over those ancient ruins at Zimbabye, and in case he finds Phœnician inscriptions he may solve the question, "Are Rider Haggard's Solomon's Mines anything more than a myth?" The Portuguese, when asked, "Who built those forts?" invariably reply, "Solomon's diggers." A Norwegian missionary who has lately visited that region observes, "I have good reason to believe that this whole coast land called Sofala is the old Ophir, called in the Septuagint Sophira and Sophara, which seems to derive its origin from the Bantu Is-ophira, or weakened through the African pronunciation (of *r* as *l*), Isofala or Sofala."

now estimated at four hundred and fifty-six thousand,[1] most of them being refugees from Zululand, where they were in danger of being accused of witchcraft and put to death. Under the wing of British power they feel secure and happy and increase rapidly. They are divided into clans, each being amenable to colonial authority. Tribal feuds and jealousies, sometimes resulting in "faction fights," which have to be put down by the strong hand of law, have proved for half a century, and are still, a safeguard against combination in opposition to the English.

Under purely native law the land belongs to the sovereign. He is monarch of all he surveys. His will is supreme. He can "eat up," that is, take away, a man's property and his life if he choose. Careful to see that none of his people becomes wealthy, he helps himself freely to their flocks. There are some laws, however, made by the national council of leading men, to which even he, it is said, is subject. It is his business to see that they are executed. The eldest son of his first wife is considered the rightful heir to the throne. The Zulus cherish and manifest a deep respect for those who have royal blood in their veins. A remarkable instance of heroic devotion to an hereditary chief is said to have occurred in Natal some years ago, which is thus told:—

"A case of succession to the chieftainship of

---

[1] This estimate is based on the total number of huts in the colony. The last census gives the white population at 44,415.

one of the tribes was decided before the local magistrate, and the hearing of the case was attended by numerous adherents of the rival claimants. After the decision, as the chiefs were returning homeward, the beaten party was suddenly overtaken by a grass fire, whereby thirteen of their number were destroyed. The young claimant to the chieftainship would have shared their fate had not one of his followers made him lie down on the ground, and covering him with his own body as a protection against the flames, he deliberately allowed himself to be burned to death, thus sacrificing his own life to save that of one whom he believed to be his legitimate chieftain."

Though the natives are poor in comparison with Europeans, and are obliged to work for the wherewithal to supply their wants, a feeling of independence is an inherited trait. To persuade them to bind themselves for a year or longer to a white man is somewhat difficult. The reason is, when harvest comes, singing, dancing, marriage feasts, and other joyful events take place at their kraals, and they must be there to participate in them. Just when the crop of sugar cane needs cutting and carting to the mill, Zulu lads often say to the planter, "Our presence is required at home." Zulu lads, however, in considerable numbers, attach themselves to their employers and make reliable servants.

That the traffic in tea, sugar, and other commodities in which Europeans are engaged may not suffer, coolies are imported from India at an expense of £28 per head, the importer paying £20 and the colonial government the balance. After five years of service they can return home passage free, or remain, which many prefer to do. Between thirty thousand and forty thousand are now in the colony. As a rule they are thrifty and industrious, and monopolize the trade of market gardening. I regret to say that there is no law prohibiting them from purchasing ardent spirits, and intemperance is their principal vice. They are sometimes detected in selling rum secretly to the natives in their kraals.

Arabs from Zanzibar and Bombay are also finding South Africa a fine field for enterprise, and there is scarcely a town or village in which their stores are not seen. Indeed the retail trade in native goods is almost wholly in their hands, to the chagrin and grief of European merchants. Both Arabs and Indians are regarded by many as a curse, but how to get rid of them is a question. Thus there will be an Asiatic as well as African problem to be settled some day in that part of the world.

The Zulus were once reduced to starvation and cannibalism in consequence of the raids of Chaka's army through the country. An incident is related of a lad who was taken prisoner but escaped in a clever manner. The cannibals, seeing a saucer-shaped earthen vessel, told the lad to carry it, remarking, "That will make a lid for the pot in which you are to be boiled." Coming to a lake full of sea cows, the boy, concluding that the companionship of those animals was preferable to that of cannibals, made a rush into the water amid a shower of spears, none of which touched him, dove and swam till he came to some reeds, among which he concealed himself, thus eluding search. He was near enough, however, to hear one of them say, "He was the fattest of the lot." That Zulu is now living and is about ninety years of age.

CHAPTER XXII.

ZULU CHARACTERISTICS.

IN bodily strength Zulus surpass the Indian and average European. The heavy burdens they carry often attract attention. An Englishman, seeing a woman about to raise to her head a load which he felt sure he could not lift, said, "You don't think you can carry that, do you?" She replied, "Were I a man I could not, but I am a woman." I have watched gangs of fifty or more young men carrying on their backs huge sacks of acacia bark, weighing not far from two hundred pounds, and rolling them into the hold of a steamship, apparently not suffering in the least from the effort.

For swiftness in running, as well as power of endurance, they are remarkable. For years men were employed by the Natal government to transport ponderous mail bags from the seaport to the colonial capital, a distance of fifty miles. Leaving at sundown, they might be seen the next morning on the steps of the post office, bright and happy, and ready, after a few hours' rest, to return with the same speed. They travel with bare feet, and their soles, being thickened by constant use over rough roads, possess emphatically a pecuniary advantage over leather.

In good health, the result of simple food and moderate exercise, the natives are proof against a multitude of ills incident to a state of civilization. It is said that two girls were once taken from a heap of dead bodies after a bloody battle, one having twenty, the other nineteen spear wounds, and both recovered. I once had a boy in my employ, through whose body a spear had been thrust, and though not as strong as many, he performed a considerable amount of labor. Several times I was called to take out pieces of skull that had been broken by knob-kerries in a quarrelsome beer drink, and the wounded places healed after a short time. Rarely did we see cases of deformity, contracted chests, weak spines, or bent shoulders.

In contrasting Zulus with American negroes I perceive a marked difference. The former, as a race, are taller and more muscular, with loftier foreheads, higher cheekbones, and a pleasanter expression of countenance. Their lips are not so thick, nor are their noses so flat. In color some of them bear a striking resemblance, but among the Zulus, Arabic features, not seen in other dark-skinned African races, are occasionally distinguishable.

At their homes the men are neat and tidy, in their way, bathing frequently, washing their hands after every meal and before milking. They invariably rinse their teeth after eating, which accounts for their clean, ivory-like appearance. Having good appetites, they often gorge themselves like pythons. Barrow, an African traveler, tells us of an ox being eaten by ten Zulus, "all but the hind legs, in three days."

This is a mild statement. In several instances when I knew an ox had been killed in the morning, I have tried to get a piece of beef in the afternoon, and have been horrified to learn that a small party of natives had eaten all but the head and hoofs. A pioneer missionary to Zululand once wrote that five or six of his servants began to eat a good-sized pig at evening, and before they slept the largest part of it was devoured.

The mode of cooking is simple. A long piece of meat is fastened to a sharp-pointed stick, placed upon the fire, and when sufficiently roasted one takes his knife, cuts off a large mouthful, and passes it on to his neighbor, and he to another. This operation is repeated till all are served. They eat some parts of an ox raw, seizing them as soon as it is killed.

In their intercourse with one another the Zulus have a well-defined code of politeness. On meeting, their salutation is "*Sa ku bonum ngani* (I see you)." The question then follows, "*Uhlezi kahle na* (Are you well)?" then the snuffbox, the token of friendship as well as *sine qua non* of comfort, is passed round. No Zulu is allowed to go out of a hut back first. In ignorance of this, I once crept out of a chief's dwelling in that way. He immediately called me back, saying, "Were you not a white man who knows no better manners, I would fine you for this breach of etiquette."

They have a curious custom called *ukuhlonipa* (shame). In accordance with it, the wife never calls her husband by his proper name, but, if he has a son, always the *father of that son*. A wife carefully avoids uttering any word occurring in the names of the principal members of her husband's family. For instance, if she has a brother-in-law named Unkomo, she will not use the word *inkomo*, meaning a cow, but some other. Formerly a native would not use a word similar to the name of a king, for fear of losing his life. For example, *impande* means the root of a tree. This is so much like Umpande, the name of the late Zulu sovereign, that no one ventured to use it. The newly married husband is careful to avoid looking at his mother-in-law, and should she be coming toward him he always takes another path or conceals himself in a cluster of bushes. No Zulu is permitted to marry a blood relation. Like the Jews, a man is expected to take the widow of a deceased brother; but to marry a cousin is to them most reprehensible.

Confidence placed in Zulu servants is seldom betrayed. Thieving is not one of their characteristics. Small bodies of men are employed yearly in transporting bags of gold and silver from the magistrate's tent, where the hut tax has been collected, twenty miles or more from a European village, and I have never heard that a shilling has been stolen. For the first thirty years of my residence among them I never considered it necessary to fasten a door or window, for fear of burglars or thieves. Missing an axe, while building my house in 1850, I suspected a native who was working with me, but in taking up the floor of my dining room two years after I found the missing article. The absence of pilfering among the Zulus I attribute to the rigid laws of the country from which they came, for in Zululand theft has from time immemorial been punishable with death. When Dingaan was on the throne, Rev. Aldin Grout took into his country a load of household goods, and wishing to leave them there while he returned to Natal for another load, he said to the headman of a kraal: "Please see, while I am gone, that none of my things are stolen." "Stolen!" said the man. "Where did you come from, that you make such a request? *We have law here.*" A Zulu was once asked by a trader whether a parcel of beads could be deposited with safety in a certain unprotected place, and received this answer: "If a man steals in Zululand, he eats no more corn." Travelers who by mistake left articles in a kraal generally found Zulus running after them to deliver them up.

I regret to say that a change has taken place in this respect. With the influx of foreigners intemperance has increased, with its attendant evils, and property is not so safe as formerly. Thanks however to the stringent prohibitory laws in Natal, the sad spectacle is not witnessed of natives lying about in a state of intoxication, as is said to be the case in Cape Town and Kimberly. But grave fears are entertained that the young Natal Zulus, who go to the gold fields in the Transvaal, will return to their homes demoralized by rum-drinking habits.

A love of fun is a prominent Zulu characteristic. They frequently crack jokes of a practical nature. Some raw natives from Zululand were about to visit their relatives, who were working for a sugar planter in the colony. The latter, desiring a little fun, met the newcomers a short distance from the planter's house, and said to them, " Our master is a great king. You must approach him on your hands and knees, just as you do Umpande, and salute him with high-sounding titles." They carried out the program faithfully, to the great amusement of the white man as well as to that of the joke players.

A Zulu lad, once seeing a woman with a pumpkin on her head, came up suddenly and inquired, apparently in great terror, " What's that on your head?" Thinking it might be a snake, she let the pumpkin fall, whereupon the roguish boy picked it up and ran away.[1]

I once " April fooled " a good natured wagon driver as we were on a journey. A few hours afterwards he asked me how we should cross a river which we were approaching. " By the *bridge*, of course," I replied. " But," said he, " have you not heard that the bridge was car-

[1] Wood's Uncivilized Races.

ried away in a late flood?" "No," I replied in an anxious tone. "Nor have I," said he, his eyes twinkling with fun.

A more gregarious and social people it is difficult to find. The young men dislike to eat alone. Rather than do so they prefer to half starve themselves. When out at service, and the economical mistress has measured out just enough Indian meal for their own mush, if a friend steps in at the time of eating, a spoon is immediately handed to him, and the mush disappears frequently before they have made "a good square meal."

A few natives raise tobacco in their kraals, but the majority refuse to do so, saying, "We would cultivate it if our neighbors did, but they are too lazy. It is therefore of no use for us to plant it, because they would come and finish it at once." This disinclines them to make efforts for the supply of their own wants. Industry and forethought are not Zulu traits, at least not of the men. A Zulu may be often heard saying to the Indian coolies, thin, haggard, hard-working people, "Why do you toil so? You are worse than white men. Look at me. See how easily I take life. I only work till I have bought a wife, and then she works for me!"

Some have said, "Zulus have no gratitude." It is a great mistake. Many instances might be related in which a thankful spirit has been manifested, and gifts bestowed for favors received. Sympathy for neighbors in trouble, especially the sick or bereaved, is a marked characteristic. Work, however important, is at once suspended that they may help their afflicted friends. Tears that roll down their cheeks as they stand around the grave of a beloved missionary belie the statement that the "natives have no feeling." Their affections are tender, and it is pleasant to see how the men fondle and nurse young children. It is only the war passion that excites them beyond all control. It has been remarked that "after living a long time with Europeans they become sour and morose." I have not seen that effect produced. On the contrary, servants of long standing have appeared to me remarkably cheerful.

In debate, of which they are very fond, they often show remarkable skill. In arguing a case they will split hairs equal to a Philadelphia lawyer. It is interesting to listen to their arguments, which roll out with amazing volubility and ease. They generally assemble under a large tree, forming a semicircle, the chief or judge sitting in front. While one is speaking, others observe silence, awaiting their turn with patience. They commence slowly and deliberately, but as they warm with the subject they rise from the ground, snap their fingers, raise the voice to the highest pitch, and become fearfully excited. All join in the discussion, and from the babel of voices a stranger would think that a fight was inevitable. After the case has been settled, the decision is generally accepted by both parties as final, the loser, not vindictive, quietly going to his home; and if he meet his rival the next day, stopping to snuff and chat with him as if nothing unpleasant had occurred.

An amusing example is thus related, in Wood's Uncivilized Races, of a cross-examination at a Zulu trial: —

"Some natives had been detected in eating an ox, and the owner brought them before a council, demanding punishment. Their defense was that they had not killed the animal, but found it dying from a wound inflicted by another ox, and so had considered it fair spoil. When the defense had been completed an old Zulu began to examine the various speakers, and as usual commenced with a question apparently wide of the subject.

"'Does an ox tail grow up, down, or sideways?'

"'Downward.'

"'Do its horns grow up, down, or sideways?'

"'Up.'

"'If an ox gores another, does he not lower his head and gore upward?'

"'Yes.'

"'Could he not gore downward?'

"'No.'

"The wily interrogator then forced the unwilling witness to examine the wound, which he asserted to have been made by the horn of another ox, and to admit that the slain beast had been stabbed, not gored."

That low cunning and deceit are often practiced among them as among other uncivilized races, we have painful evidence; but, as one truthfully observes, "The wonder is not that these evils and perversions exist, but that, in the absence for ages of all revealed truth and all proper religious instruction, there should still remain so much of mental integrity, so much ability to discern truth and justice, and withal so much regard for these principles in their daily intercourse with one another."

Before the advent of Europeans with the arts of civilization considerable ingenuity was displayed in manufacturing spears, hoes, or picks from iron mined out of their own soil. Their forges and anvils were of the crudest description, but they managed to do their work creditably. They also made rings from an amalgam of copper and iron. Their dishes for cooking, carrying water or beer, baskets, and beer-strainers, milkpails, wooden pillows, spoons, etc., show considerable skill. In making skins soft and pliable they are quite equal to furriers in civilized lands. In the medical art some of them are skilled in healing certain diseases by the use of roots and herbs which abound in the country.

They have an ingenious process for making a fire. A dry reed is taken about six inches long, a notch cut near the middle, in which is rotated between the palms of the hands a small hard stick. One is reminded of a carpenter's drill. Soon the hot ashes appear, from which a flame is secured.

Zulu lads acquire the industrial arts with facility. In blacksmithing, shoemaking, wagon-making, and printing, they can compete with white men if properly trained. I had a native printer who composed with rapidity, and printed a newspaper in the Zulu language. He was also a bookbinder. In learning to read, the children are quite as apt as the whites. In vocal music, some of them are quite proficient. In mental and physical ability they do not seem to be inferior to the Anglo-Saxon race. As civilizing agencies have enlightened other tribes, the same agencies, if faithfully applied, will raise the Zulus, also, to a like state of advancement.

CHAPTER XXIII.

ZULU WEDDINGS AND FUNERALS.

THE natives look forward to a marriage occasion with joy, for it is a time to revel in dancing and feasting. If in high life, the greater the glee, the greater the quantity of beef to be consumed, the larger the potations of beer. A king's wedding generally lasts six or seven days. Being present at the marriage of Cetywayo, the late Zulu chief, when he took to himself his fifteenth wife, the excitement I witnessed was almost beyond bounds. Spectators, quite a thousand in number, sat on the ground (for there were no seats), looking at the five hundred or more men and women engaged in their tumultuous dance, and appeared to be thoroughly fascinated. After fifteen minutes I should have left, had I not made an engagement to meet his sable majesty at the close of the ceremony. On this occasion the bride, for some reason or other, was seated by herself, but the fourteen wives were together, directly in front of a brother missionary and myself. The obesity of these African queens attracted our attention. We estimated that each would weigh at least two hundred pounds. Such an amount of avoirdupois in human flesh, possessed by one man, I never before witnessed.

I was told that they did little or no work, ate an enormous quantity of beef, and drank as much beer as they could. As the hot sun began to beat down on my head, I lifted up my umbrella for shade, when one of the king's wives requested the use of it for a short time. I complied, but when I politely called for it, she refused to give it up. Now was my time to give an African queen a lecture on politeness, which was not without effect, for the umbrella was soon returned.

Cetywayo, the leader in the dance, was dressed like the majority of the men, with skins of wild animals about his loins, and the only way I could distinguish him from others was by a long feather stuck to the gutta-percha-like ring on his head. That feather is used only by royalty on marriage occasions. The dance, if such it can be called, was one of the noisiest demonstrations conceivable, consisting simply in stamping the ground forcibly, swinging the hands up and down, chanting a variety of tunes, shouting and screaming, howling and yelling, the perspiration dropping like rain from the half-nude bodies.

When at the greatest pitch of excitement, I remarked to my companion, "If these Zulus ever come into collision with British authority, and display the same enthusiasm in war as they do on this festive occasion, they will prove no despicable foe." In the "Zulu war," some years after, they fought like tigers.

Now that Zulu girls under English protection are not obliged to marry, *nolens volens*, they enjoy a privilege which some in more civilized countries might regard as advantageous, that of " popping the question," or selecting husbands from among the old or young men, according to their fancy. Every year with them is " leap year." They sometimes choose those who are not inclined to reciprocate their affection, but, nothing daunted, they persevere until they succeed. In Wood's Uncivilized Races we read of a Zulu girl who fell ardently in love with a young chief as he was displaying his agility in a dance. " He did not know her, and was rather surprised when she presented herself at his kraal and avowed the state of her affections. He, however, did not return them, and as the girl refused to leave, he was obliged to send for her brother, who removed her by force. She soon made her way back again, and this time was severely beaten for her pertinacity. The stripes had no effect on her, and in less than a week she again presented herself. Finding that his sister was so determined, the brother suggested that the too fascinating chief had better marry the girl and so end the dispute, and the result was that at last she gained her point, the needful cows were paid and the marriage took place."

Zulu courtship often goes on for some time without the knowledge of the parents. The girls are not in a hurry to be married, knowing well that the happiest period of their life is that of their youth. Many of them, however, are mere flirts. When fifteen or sixteen years old, their fathers, hankering for cattle, begin to chide, saying, "Is it not time you were married? This flirtation must come to an end." Finding that her father and brothers are seeking some one to recommend to her as a husband, she suddenly disappears, having hied away to her lover's kraal. In case the parents have no objection to the family, and they are sure that within a reasonable time the required cattle for payment will be forthcoming, they do not interfere, knowing that initiatory steps for the marriage will follow. In a day or two there appear at the home of the future bride a party of men driving two or three cows. They have come to negotiate for the proposed union. The usual friendly custom of taking snuff is gone through with, the bargain is ratified, the cows left as first instalment, and the visitors go home apparently satisfied. What follows I give in the language of one who is more intimately acquainted with native customs than myself: —

"Both parties have new songs and dances to learn, and it is a matter of emulation which shall excel. The bride has by her a stock of mats, spoons, dishes, etc., which she has collected, with which to begin housekeeping. Her father's gift is a blanket, and cattle according to his rank. But no girl ever goes to her husband without an ox, which is ever looked upon afterward as the ox of the *amahlozi* (ancestral spirits), the loss of which by death would be considered a token of desertion by the protecting spirits of her father's house, and the slaughter of which, in the event of any calamity (such as disease or barrenness), is an acceptable sacrifice.

"When the eventful day has arrived, the bride and party (the higher the rank the more the followers) set out for the bridegroom's kraal, which, however, they will not enter until night, singing and dancing as they go. Early in the morning they go to the nearest stream, wash and dress, and about noon come up and begin the dance, the bridegroom's party looking on. When both sides have finished, which may or may not be on the first day, a cow is slaughtered by the bridegroom and given to the bride's party.

"At night the girl wanders about the kraal, followed by her own sex, relatives of the bridegroom. She is 'crying for her father's house,' where she was well treated. Now she has come to a strange household where she may be ill used, and where she has only the certainty of hard work. She is supposed to be trying to run away, and the girls to be preventing her. Next day the bridegroom, his brother, sisters, and friends take their seat in the cattle fold, and the second and last part of the ceremony, called *ukuhlambisa*, takes place. (Ukuhlambisa means to give wherewithal to wash the hands. Perhaps it is a symbol that on that day she has washed away all her old life.) The bride comes in with her party of girls, carrying in her hand a spear, which, by the way, she has carried all the time. One girl bears a dish of water and a calabash, and another some beads. Then coming up, singing and dancing, the bride throws the water over her husband. She also sprinkles her brother and sister in law, striking the latter as a symbol that from that time she assumes authority over the girls in her husband's household. After this is done she breaks the staff of the spear, and makes a run for the gate of the kraal, as a last effort to get away. If she is not stopped by a young man appointed for the purpose, it is a great disgrace, and the husband has to pay a cow to get her back. The marriage rites are then finished. No widow, remarried, breaks the staff of the spear.

"For some time after marriage the wife will not drink any sour milk. She was purchased with milk-giving cattle, and cannot eat her own purchase price. But after a while she takes the broken spear to her old home and returns with a goat, or sheep, or cow, which is slaughtered, the defiling principle going out of the milk into the dead animal. Henceforth she may drink the milk. In Zulu language she has 'cleansed her spoon.'"

Marriage customs vary somewhat, but the above is a fair description of the average. Traveling once on horseback through a thickly populated part of Natal, I came unexpectedly on a procession of natives, in front of whom a large ox was being driven, and was told that it was the winding up of a wedding ceremony. Having dismounted and turned my horse out to graze, I watched the proceedings. When the procession reached the gate of the bridegroom's kraal, the bride was closely veiled by her female attendants, nor was the veil removed till she had taken her place in the ring for the final dance. A hundred or more natives engaged in it with all the energy of which they were capable, their bodies covered with perspiration, but I could not see the bridegroom anywhere. On inquiring as to his whereabouts, I received the reply, "Wait a few minutes and you will see." It turned out that he was seated near myself among the spectators, and apparently as unconcerned as any of them. After a little, the bride left the ring, dancing and singing like the rest, but evidently in search of somebody or something. Suddenly she appeared and placed her hand heavily on her lover's head. This the Zulus call *ukuketa*, or choosing a husband. It was a signal that she had selected him in this public manner as her partner for life. The favored individual immediately jumped up, and went into his own hut in the kraal to prepare for his part in the dance. When he again appeared he looked like a new being covered with the skins of various animals, beads and brass ornaments in great profusion. Taking his place in the ring, he danced as enthusiastically as the rest.

What attracted my attention particularly was an occurrence that usually takes place at the close of every wedding. The father of the bride took a shield, and, standing in front of the dancers, who for the time kept quiet, made a speech in which he praised in no qualified terms his daughter, dilated on all he had done for her, said the number of cows he had received was too small, hoped she would meet with good treatment, prove a fruitful vine, etc. Occasionally he emphasized his words by jumping up and kicking his shield with violence. Then the father of the bridegroom appeared on the scene, also bearing a shield, lauding his son to the skies, complaining that he had paid too many cattle, that the girl was homely in appearance, not strong enough to do much work, emphasizing his remarks in the same manner as the bride's father had done. This, it is said, is done that the bride may not be unduly elated. The crowd then dispersed, singing and shouting vociferously. The wife, for some weeks after marriage, unless it is the planting season, does no work. When she does take up her daily duties she finds often by sad experience that the happiest days of her life were those when she was a girl at home.

I have described the marriage of uncivilized Zulus. When they abandon heathenism and live on mission stations they are married according to Christian rites. It was feared by some that a colonial law lately enacted, making natives married in a Christian manner liable to punishment if they took other wives, would lessen the number of Christian marriages, but I am told it is not the case.

So large are the assemblies which gather on

marriage occasions that it is impossible for them to find sitting or standing room in our places of worship. I remember once going to an out-station to marry a couple, and finding several hundred heathen people who had come to witness the ceremony. It was performed in the open air, and it was rather difficult to keep the crowd quiet during its performance. Previous to the marriage a procession was formed at the house of the bridegroom by the clad Zulus, to escort the happy pair to the place where they were to be united, and as they appeared in sight on the brow of an adjacent hill several young people shouted, "Behold, the bridegroom cometh; let us go forth to meet him!" quite in imitation of the old custom in the land of the Bible.

After the marriage ceremony was performed, a hymn was sung, and the procession, headed by the bride and bridegroom, started for their future home, with flags flying, the beat of a drum, and the occasional discharge of a musket. Had I wished, it would have been impossible to restrain the hilarity and noisy demonstrations of the multitude, and for two hours they beat the ground with their canes and clapped their hands and shouted till their lungs were hoarse. The louder the noise, the happier they seemed to be. I saw nothing, however, reprehensible in their conversation and conduct.

Singing matches are common at Zulu Christian weddings. The chief object seems to be to ascertain which party will sing the longest, and they often continue till midnight.

Funeral ceremonies among the Zulus are few. On the death of an aged person there is no demonstration of grief. They say he or she has "gone home." But the reverse is the case if the deceased is a young man or a man in the prime of life. Then the people in the vicinity repair to the house of mourning, and for days and nights naught is heard but the doleful wail carrying sadness to many hearts. Often at midnight we have been roused from slumber by loud cries and wailing nearly a mile from our dwelling. One reason why all the heathen neighbors are in the habit of visiting the bereaved kraal to condole with its inmates is a fear of being suspected, and even charged with having in some way caused the calamity in case they do not attend. The dead are generally buried in a sitting posture, and into the grave are thrown blankets, mats, spoons, the ornaments worn and tools used by the individual when alive. When the grave is nearly covered, a large number of stones is thrown in, and then a mound two or three feet high is made. Zulus, as a general rule, have very little regard for the sepulchers of their countrymen, except those of kings. It has been the custom in Zululand, and probably is now, in some parts of South Africa not reached by civilization and Christianity, when a king dies, to bury with him some of his servants, cupbearers, milkmen, etc., that the saying may be fulfilled, "The king must not go to the place of the dead alone." The unfortunate individuals selected were generally strangled, and their bodies placed at the bottom of the grave, the royal corpse being laid upon them. It is reported that some have entered the grave alive, and died with perfect submission. One would think that those suspecting their probable fate would try to escape, but I have been told that this is not the case. A kind of fatalism takes possession of them, which is characteristic of the Zulus. They say, " It was predestinated we should die in this manner," or they may imagine they will be happier in the other world if they accompany their sovereign. The English have put a stop to the cruel custom, and, in one case, Christian teaching also had a similar effect. Rev. J. Allsopp, a missionary of my acquaintance, visited the son of a chief who had died, and ten or twelve individuals would have been slain, had it not been for the missionary's intercession. His account of it is as follows:—

"The young chief said, ' My father is dead. Who will guide and tell me what I shall do?' We stood for a little, when, in grief he asked, 'Will you go and see my father?' I said, ' Yes.' I was taken to the hut, in which the chief was sitting, not lying, dead, with his blanket thrown over him. I removed the covering, looked upon his face, and left the hut. I went back and found the young chief still standing. He put out his hand again, and I took it as before. Then I said: 'Now is the day of your power, What will you do? Shall the news go from this place to-day to all throughout South Africa and across the sea, to those Christians who send you your missionaries, and to the Queen of England, that you have used your power to-day in taking life and shedding blood? Shall it be said that you have stained your hands, and that they are red with the blood of your subjects? Or shall the word go forth that you are a man of mercy; that you have heard the gospel; that you know something of what you ought to do? Give me your word.' He looked me steadily in the face, and said, ' Umfundisi (Missionary), not a man shall die.' I took him again by the hand, and said, ' Farewell. I believe you. The chief has spoken: not a man shall die.'

"I returned home, and learned only a few hours afterward that, in the assembly of two or three hundred who were already grouped behind the cattle kraal, some nine or ten were pointed out to be slain in a few minutes, but they were not slain. The chief sent for the men, and said, "You know that the old councilors and the witch doctors would have you die; but I say, Go and live upon such a hill; there you will be safe, and nobody shall harm you."

And so it was. The gospel has its effect; and when it teaches men to value life as they never valued it before, and when it teaches the heathen to value their wives and children as they never valued them before, it is doing something.

These are some of the effects which are manifest to our eyes who are laboring amongst the heathen. Who will not rejoice in such saving power?

On closing the grave of a king an immense heap of stones is placed upon it, and the national dirge, used only at royal funerals, is chanted, while at the same time all the men present strike their shields with knob-kerries most vehemently. The grave is closely watched for weeks, sometimes months, to prevent wizards from stealing the body, which is supposed to work charms and even miracles.

In the case of the decease of a common person the most shameful haste is sometimes exercised in the burial. A woman of my acquaintance was taken to the place of interment late one night, and was so lightly covered that, to the astonishment of her son, who went early the next morning to complete the burial, she said to him as she sat up in the grave, "How do you do, my child?"

When aid is rendered to strangers in performing the last rites, pay is always demanded. A cow and a calf, with a goat for the "washing of the hands," has been the standard fee from time immemorial. Before the light of the gospel began to shine among them it was common to drag old people who appeared to be near their end to some secluded place, and there let them die alone, their corpses becoming the prey of wild beasts and vultures. The dead bodies of criminals shared the same fate.

CHAPTER XXIV.

ZULU KINGS AND WARS.

CHAKA, the most renowned of Zulu kings, not improperly called the "Bonaparte of South Africa," began to reign about the beginning of this century. His name awakens deep emotions in the native mind. As it is little more than fifty years since his death, there are natives living who knew him personally, and they are never tired of rehearsing his mighty deeds. I have often heard them repeat with genuine delight a song which his warriors were accustomed to sing to his praise: —

> Thou hast finished the nations.
> Where wilt thou go to battle now?
> Hey! where wilt thou go to battle now?

Unlike other South African chiefs, he was in the habit of fighting in person at the head of his braves, and it is said he never fled before a foe or lost a battle. His name is regarded by the Zulus as sacred, and is never mentioned except to give solemnity to an oath or to nerve the warrior for battle. At the time of his death he had a standing army of thirty-six regiments. "In working out the scheme of his ambition he introduced some remarkable reforms into the art of barbarian warfare. Each regiment was distinguished from others by the color and pattern of their shields. His men were taught to wield the short assegai and shield in close personal combat, instead of putting their trust, as of old, in the long javelin hurled from afar; and the warrior who returned from the fight without assegai and shield in his hand, or who bore the mark of a wound on his back, did so to the forfeit of his life. His warriors were forbidden to marry, as domestic ties were thought to soften and enervate. But after a certain period of service old regiments were superannuated as veterans and furnished with wives, and new levies raised to take their places in the ranks."[1]

During the reign of Chaka, which lasted only nineteen years, he extended his conquests far and wide, and swept away no less than three hundred tribes, slaying all who would not submit to his authority.

His nature was cruel. He stabbed his own mother to the heart, and then called on the nation to mourn her death. At an assembly of his leading men he was once speaking of a tribe he was about to attack, and he laid a wager that their dead bodies would fill a certain ravine. The tribe was slain; but the king's wager was lost, for the ravine was not filled.

When in the zenith of his power, he allowed a few Englishmen to settle at Port Natal, commissioning two of their number to go to England with the following message to George IV: "If you will look after your interests in Eng-

[1] See Dr. Robert Mann's book on "Colony of Natal."

land, I will look after mine in Africa, and will take care that no enemies are left. We will be the sovereigns of the world."

Captain Allen Gardiner, a philanthropic gentleman, who went to South Africa during Chaka's reign, received the king's permission to live at the Port, on condition that he would send back to Zululand all refugees from that country. The captain agreed, and soon a party of men were sent bound to Chaka with the request that he would spare their lives. They were shut up in a hut and left to die of starvation. It is a curious coincidence that the good, but indiscreet captain was starved to death in Terra del Fuego, where he had gone to evangelize the Patagonians.

The soldiers who fought under Chaka were the fathers and grandfathers of those who resisted so valiantly an army of British troops, sweeping away an entire regiment on that sad morning of January 22, 1879, at Isandhlwana. English officers, who had witnessed battles in other lands, often remarked that they never saw courage displayed equal to that of the Zulus.

Like most African chiefs, Chaka fell at the hands of assassins. Three of his own brothers rushed into his kraal one day, and seeing him unprotected stabbed him with assegais, and are said to have drunk on the spot the gall of the chief they had conspired to assassinate. Chaka, as he was about to expire, is reported to have uttered these prophetic words, "You kill me; but the white race, a race you do not know, shall occupy this land." His prophecy is fulfilled. Not a stone's throw from his grave, where were once heard the songs of bloodthirsty barbarians, stands a church in which English Christians worship.

On the death of Chaka, Dingaan, his brother and one of the conspirators, ascended the throne. He was more wily and cruel, even more like Nero, than his predecessor. Captain Gardiner, who visited him in 1835, saw him amusing himself by torturing one of his menservants. Commanding him to hold out his arm, he seized his hand, and with his burning glass, the gift of a white man, he burnt a hole into his skin. The poor servant writhed with pain, but dared not utter a word lest something worse should befall him. One of his titles — a fit one — was "Hyena-man." It is said he would never acknowledge that he had any children. An infant was once brought to him with the hope that its life might be spared. Captain Gardiner remarked: "He instantly seized his own child by the heels and with one blow deprived it of that life which, with such a father, it could have been no privilege to enjoy. This horrid deed was only surpassed by the immediate murder of the agonized mother, whose eyes closed with the vivid impression of the scene she had beheld."

The Dutch farmers in South Africa will never cease to execrate the name of that tyrant, when they recall his treatment of their fathers. In 1830, seventy strong, athletic

Boers, well armed and mounted, visited Dingaan, for the purpose of making a treaty with him, and obtaining a part of his country. Some of them, to obtain his favor, had previously, at his request, attacked a distant native tribe, obnoxious to him, stripped them of their cattle and presented them to him. The party was received with apparent cordiality, their request complied with, and a large slice of Zululand ceded to them. Elated with success, they were about to return to their families in Natal, when a polite invitation came to them from his sable majesty to tarry a little, take a friendly drink of beer, and witness a war dance, which he was arranging for their amusement. This request was coupled with another, that they should leave their guns and ammunition outside of his kraal, that the people might not be afraid. Alas! the unsuspecting Boers had not calculated on the treachery of their host. They repaired to the place designated, and, while gazing on the weird scene of thousands of savages engaged in the dance, Dingaan suddenly arose, waved his hand, and said, "Kill the wizards." The order was executed, and in less than fifteen minutes every farmer was beaten to death with knob-kerries and canes. I have conversed with natives who took part in that massacre, and they said the Boers fought desperately with their hunting-knives, the only weapons they had, and quite as many Zulus perished as Dutch. The corpses of the latter were dragged out to a Zulu golgotha, where they became a prey for wild beasts and birds.

Without narrating in detail what followed, suffice it to say, the friends of the murdered Boers wreaked fearful vengeance on Dingaan; defeated his army and, at last, placed Umpande, his brother, on the Zulu throne. Dingaan, when in the zenith of his power, had desired to slay Umpande, thinking that he might become a rival, but, through the intervention of a friend, spared him, remarking, however, "You wish me to spare a dog which will one day bite me." Driven out of Zululand by the Dutch, Dingaan sought protection among the Amaswazi people, to whom he had shown no compassion, and it is not strange that they quickly terminated his existence. Thus there was fulfilled a Zulu proverb, "The swimmer in the end gets carried away with the stream."

Umpande was not inclined to war, and for thirty years kept on good terms with both Dutch and English. That there were times when his young braves desired to invade Natal, enrich themselves with cattle, and sweep away the few white people residing there, and that they could easily have done it, is evident. But Umpande, supported by his old men, always refused to gratify them. Once, when they manifested considerable anger because not allowed to attack the English, an old councilor, Ulukwasi, by name, made the following eloquent speech:—

"I am old and am almost inclined to feel

that in speaking to you young warriors on the present subject, I demean myself, for you are but children in many ways. I fought under Chaka with my single assegai, and let my companions in arms say whether my assegai ever came back bright as I took it from home, or if I ever turned from the foe. I have stood under Dingaan's rule, with bullets from the guns of the Dutch passing around me like bees, and the wounds I show bear witness for me. You speak of battles to come: I deal with those already fought, into which we went a host and returned few in numbers. You ask to be led against the English? Why? Are they enemies? You cannot fight with friends, so they must be enemies. I will tell you in what their hostility consists. You were cold, and they gave you blankets. You wanted ornaments, and they brought you beads and other things, for which, in fair trade, you gave your cattle. Did they steal those cattle, that you want to plunder them? Tell me of one instance in which an Englishman has stolen a Zulu beast, and I will join you in your raid; but, if you cannot, then tell me when you start, and I, together with my family, will cross over to the English."[1]

This speech is said to have saved Natal, but it cost the speaker his life. It was not long before he died, probably from poison.

The successor of Umpande was Cetywayo, one of his youngest sons. The old king desired that Umbulazi, his oldest son, should have the

[1] "Zululand and the Zulus," by Fred B. Finney.

supremacy, and did not hesitate to express his wish to the nation; but Cetywayo, a cunning fellow and burning with ambition, succeeded in winning over to his side the majority of the people. The father saw no other way than to allow the sons to settle the question of sovereignty by force of arms. Evidently Umbulazi had some misgivings in regard to the issue of the contest, for he selected a place for the engagement only five miles from the Tugela River, which divides Zululand from Natal, hoping, in case of defeat, his adherents might escape into that colony.

The fight was one of the most sanguinary that ever occurred among the Zulus. Umbulazi was defeated, and is supposed to have been slain, as he was never afterwards seen. Multitudes ran to the river with the intention of crossing, but were speared on the way, mothers with babes on their backs as well as the men. Many were drowned, as the river was swollen at the time. Cetywayo was "master of the situation," and the whole Zulu nation acknowledged him as supreme chief.

Although the Zulus are a nation of warriors, and unsurpassed for courage in battle, yet when not on the "warpath," they are as orderly and peaceful a tribe as can anywhere be found. For the past fifty years those residing in Natal have been loyal subjects, only one case of rebellion having occurred and that very quickly ended.

In the government of the natives, Natal has

been exceedingly fortunate in having, for thirty years or more, Sir Theophilus Shepstone as secretary for native affairs, a gentleman whom all, black and white, could love and trust. That peace has been preserved for so long a time is owing largely to his able and wise management. His father was a missionary in Kaffraria. When young, he attached himself to the staff of Benjamin D'Urban, an English officer, and was engaged in the Kaffir war of 1835. Ten years later he came to Natal and began that career of usefulness, the noble record of which will fill a prominent place in colonial history. He has always been ready to aid Christian missionaries by counsel and otherwise. The Natal Zulus felt that in "Somseu," as they called their white king, they had a kind and judicious "father."

"Could the Zulu war of 1878–79 have been avoided?" is a question often asked, to which various replies have been given. My own opinion at the time was, and it has not changed, that Natal was in imminent danger, and that if the English had not taken measures to curb the war passion in Zululand a raid would have taken place, the results of which would have been fearful in the extreme.

Cetywayo, though he may have been disposed, personally, to live in peace with his white neighbors, could not control his young braves. They were determined, as they said, "to go somewhere and wash their spears in blood." Moreover they had come into possession of firearms, and were anxious to try them. Not permitted to attack native tribes on their border, they began to think and proudly talk of invading Natal. Travelers, traders, and missionaries saw, from the impudence displayed, that mischief was brewing.

The Zulus were really under obligations to the English. Soon after Cetywayo began his career, he was crowned by them "king of Zululand, and ally to England." Intestine strife had been averted by the wise intervention of Sir Theophilus Shepstone, Natal's representative. At the time of his coronation, Cetywayo willingly, and it was supposed sincerely, made certain promises, on the fulfillment of which, he was told, the safety of himself and country depended. Those were that he must stop the indiscriminate shedding of blood; that no Zulu should be condemned to death without a trial, and that for minor offenses loss of property should be substituted in place of death. Everything was carefully explained to him. Would that he had been wise! Soon after, when called to account for disregarding the agreement, he said, with an air of defiance, to the messenger from the Natal government: "Why do the white people start at nothing? I have not yet begun to kill. It is the custom of our nation, and I shall not depart from it. Have I not asked the English to allow me to wash my spears since the death of my father? and they have kept playing with me all this time, treating me like a child. Go back and tell the English that I shall act on my own account, and that if they wish me to agree to their laws I shall leave and become a wanderer; but it will be seen that *I shall not go without having acted.*"

At another time, he sent this message to the colonial governor: "I shall do as I like. I am king in my own country. Take care of your own affairs, and I will take care of mine."

In the ultimatum sent to him by the Natal authorities, at the advice of Sir Bartle Frere, previous to the commencement of hostilities, he was called upon to make suitable reparation for raids made by his people into the Natal territory; also, to disband his army, as well as to conform to the requirements previously imposed. He was also told that a British agent must be allowed to reside in his country; that every man when he comes to man's estate should be free to marry; that missionaries and their converts, who had left the country through fear, must be allowed to return and reoccupy their stations, etc. Setting at naught the advice of old missionaries, for whom his father had cherished respect, he listened to the proud boastings of his youthful warriors, who said, "We are not afraid of those few insignificant white men; we can easily drive them into the sea!" and suffered the thirty days' ultimatum to expire. Thereupon the British troops crossed the border and proclaimed martial law.

What wiser, better course could have been pursued? That Natal was in peril no clear-headed man can deny. The colonists were near the crater of a volcano liable at any time to an eruption. Cetywayo could not control his warriors. Fearing the result of their rashness, he remonstrated with them, but they tauntingly replied, "You are a coward; you are not the son of Chaka."

The mayor of the colonial capital, in a letter to the "Aborigines Protection Society," in England, fairly stated the matter when he said: "The real point to be met and settled is this: Is her majesty's authority, as representing peace and civilization, or Cetywayo's authority, as representing bloodshed and barbarism, to be paramount in South Africa? That is the real question, but instead of calmly discussing it, a side issue has been raised by the opponents of Sir Bartle Frere, and that is this: Could he, with safety to her majesty's dominions, have waited before sending the ultimatum to Cetywayo until he had submitted it for the consideration of her majesty's government at home? This, I admit, is a question fairly open to debate. But the question of insisting on the fulfillment of the ultimatum itself, to the letter, if the lives and property of her majesty's subjects and of her allies in South Africa were to be secured, is not a matter of debate merely, but a necessity that had to be faced. The side issue raised is merely important as a question of official subordination."

Without particularizing, I will add that the most competent judges in South Africa decided at the time, and we believe the impartial verdict of history will sustain their decision, that the Natal authorities were justified in the course they adopted, and moreover that Sir Bartle Frere, "that noble old man, and certainly the most talented high commissioner South Africa has ever seen," showed his wisdom by bringing the case to issue at once, as he did by advising the governor of Natal to send the ultimatum to Cetywayo. That having been contemned, war was inevitable.

At the commencement of hostilities one of the greatest military blunders occurred of which we have any account in English warfare. Lord Chelmsford, the general, was especially warned by those who were well acquainted with the Zulu modes of warfare, to avoid being taken by surprise. Said George Cato, American consul in Natal, an old colonist: "My lord, when you get into Zululand, keep your army together, and be ready at a moment's warning to go into laager"; that is, draw the wagons into the form of a square and chain them together, pulling horses, oxen, etc., safely inside. Mr. J. J. Mys, a Dutchman with a lifelong experience of Zulu warfare, also said to the general, a few days before the army crossed the border: "Be on your guard. I have knowledge of the deceit and treachery of the Zulu nation. The Zulus are more dangerous than you think. I lost my father and my brother through them, because we held them too cheaply. Trek[1] into Zululand with two laagers close to each other." It is said the general smiled, and observed that he thought it would not be necessary.

[1] A common word for "journey," or "go."

Confident of an easy victory, the British soldiers, with a large body of colonial volunteers and native allies, entered the country and pitched their camp at the foot of a high mountain called Isandhlwana. The day following, instead of sending out scouts in all directions, and waiting till he could be sure that there were no signs of the enemy, the general, with a part of his army, went off twelve or fifteen miles to reconnoiter. Just then there arrived on the field from twenty to thirty thousand of Cetywayo's best soldiers to meet the invaders. Instead of "going into laager," as the Dutch would have done under like circumstances, the English hastily began the fight, regardless, it is said, of orders the general had left, but which unfortunately he was not present to see executed. They soon found that the Zulus were a foe not to be despised. Rushing upon them with a fearful yell, fearless of cannon, Gatling gun, and showers of bullets which laid low at least three thousand of their number, they demolished the English camp in less than an hour's time. A regiment of "redcoats" standing in a solid body fired away all their cartridges and then, as they tried to defend themselves with their bayonets, were speared, *not one escaping*. The rest, flying in different directions, were pursued and many of them slain while attempting to reach the Natal Colony. The general, returning at dark to the place where he had left his camp, found all gone, tents, horses, oxen, mules, beds, provisions, guns, money, all that the Zulus thought would be of any use. The dead soldiers were stripped of their clothing, and the wounded, according to native custom, put to death. The feelings of Lord Chelmsford, as he stood or sat by the dead bodies of his soldiers during that long, dark night of January 22, 1879, can be better imagined than described. Report said that for six months not a smile was seen on his countenance.

As the camp was rifled of everything, and a new commissariat would be needed, a return to Natal was decided upon the next morning. A body of Zulus had crossed the Buffalo River into the colony and attacked a small fort at "Rorke's Drift," where a mere handful of Englishmen defended themselves against the enemy, although some Zulus came near enough to catch hold of the rifles, between the biscuit-boxes and bags of grain, with which the fortification was made. Returning to their own country they passed within gunshot of Lord Chelmsford's troops, who never offered to harm them, and were only too glad to find themselves in a place of safety.

The terror that seized the people in Natal, after the massacre at Isandhlwana, was so great that many of them sought protection in the towns or fortified places. The belief was general that the Zulus, elated with their success, would overrun the colony. England became alarmed, and sent out a large number of troops and the subjugation of Zululand was prosecuted in a more cautious manner.

As a result of the Zulu war, Cetywayo was taken prisoner, sent to Cape Town, his country divided, and over each division was placed a petty chief. The king, after a visit to England and an audience with her majesty the Queen, was permitted to return and resume authority over a portion of his former people. But soon a contention arose between rival chiefs. One of them, Usibepu, visited Cetywayo, after his return, and was apparently disposed to live in peace, but was snubbed by the son of Umpande, in a manner not likely to be forgotten. The "Usutu," as Cetywayo's party were called, said to him, "You are only a dog," and soon began to make raids into his territory. This roused the ire of Usibepu, who resolved to crush his insolent rival, though he should die in the attempt. With nearly a thousand picked warriors and aided by some European filibusters, who joined him in hopes of reward, he marched all one night and came suddenly at daybreak on Ondine, Cetywayo's kraal, putting all its inhabitants to an ignominious flight. It was not a battle, but a slaughter of fugitives. Abraham, a Christian native, member of the Umsunduzi church, who was visiting Ondine at that time, took the chief's rifle, and defended himself and the king as long as the cartridges lasted, and he was then shot himself. Cetywayo, after receiving a spear wound, escaped into the Inkanhla forest, from which he was rescued shortly after by a party of English troops. He soon died, probably a natural death, though his own people say from poison administered by his enemies.

His son Undinizulu, a lad of twenty years, swore that he would avenge his father's death, and in direct opposition to the English authorities, now in possession of Zululand, renewed the quarrel between the Usutu, his own party, and that of Usibepu. The result was that he was made a prisoner, tried before an English judge, and sentenced to banishment at St. Helena for ten years. There, the unfortunate prince, like the great Napoleon, will have opportunity to reflect on that turn of the wheel of fortune which deprived him of his chieftainship and terminated the Zulu dynasty.

A "Zulu Defense Committee" has been formed in England,[1] chiefly through the eloquent and importunate pleading of Miss Harriette E. Colenso, daughter of the late bishop of that name. She, it is said, has "expended more than £3.000" in defending the exiled chiefs, but, as yet, little has been accomplished except bringing the matter before the English public. The repatriation of the Zulu chiefs, it is thought by the imperial authorities, would disturb the present peaceful state of Zululand. If the exiles behave well, and the political condition of their country admits of their return with safety, I have no doubt it will be effected at an early date.

[1] See Appendix.

CHAPTER XXV.

ZULU FOLKLORE.

ZULU native lore is quite limited, all we have being taken from the lips of the people. They had an abundance of *legends*, many of which, together with their religious beliefs, have been collected and published in two volumes by Rev. Henry Callaway, M.D., a missionary bishop of the Church of England.[1] In this department he labored with unwearied zeal and perseverance, and we are indebted to him for having saved much which might otherwise have been lost.

Dr. Callaway said the belief was irresistibly fixed in his mind that the Zulu tales point out very clearly that the Zulus are a degenerated people; that they are not now in the condition, intellectually or physically, in which they were during the "legend-producing period" of their existence, but have sunk from a higher state. Like the discovered relics of giant buildings in Asia and America, they appear to speak of a mightier and better past which, it may be, is lost forever. "What we have preserved," he says, "contains evidence of intellectual powers not to be despised, while we have, scattered everywhere throughout the tales, those evidences of tender feelings, gentleness, and love,

[1] Callaway's Nursery Tales.

which should teach us that in dealing with savages we are dealing with savage *men*, who only need culture to have developed in them the finest traits of our human nature."

Elizabeth Cookson, in her "Introduction to the Legends of Manx Land," has truthfully observed: "Popular tales, songs, and superstitions are not altogether profitless; like the fingers of a clock, they point to the time of day. Turns and modes of thought, that else had set in darkness, are by them preserved and reflected, even as objects sunk below the horizon are occasionally brought again into *view* by atmospheric reflection. Fables are *facts* in so far as they mirror the minds of our less scientific ancestors."

In citing a few specimens of Zulu light literature, I begin with a fable, the moral of which is: "If you want anything done well, do it yourself."

Long ago a certain king sent for all the animals to go to a certain place and receive their tails. On the day the tails were to be distributed, the coney, not being disposed to take the journey in consequence of a little rain, said to the monkey, "When you get your tail, will you ask for mine also, and bring it to me?" The monkey agreed, but on his way home managed to join the coney's tail to his own, saying, "If he is too lazy to go for what he needs, he must go without. I shall not encourage his idleness." So the monkey has a long tail, but the coney scarcely any.

When Zulus ask others to do for them what they ought to do for themselves, they often humorously reply, "Have you forgotten the coney that lost its tail?"

Other races have fables accounting for the tailless condition of animals, such as that of the bear, in the Norse tales, fishing, at the instigation of the fox, with his tail through a hole in the ice till it was frozen, and losing it when he attempted to escape; but the fable of the coney has much more significance.

Another fable is that of The Hyena and the Moon, which is not unlike Æsop's fable of The Dog and the Shadow.

It happened on a time that a hyena found a bone and, taking it up, carried it in his mouth. The moon began to shine with a beautiful light on a river near by, and when the hyena saw the moon in the water he threw down the bone and plunged into the water to catch it, thinking it to be beef. But he caught nothing. Another hyena came and took the bone. The first hyena was much ridiculed for his fruitless plunge into the water and the loss of his bone. So the Zulus often laugh at each other when unsuccessful in their vain enterprises, saying, "You are like the hyena that threw away the bone and caught nothing."

Jack the Giant Killer, or rather a compound of that hero and Tom Thumb, is found in Zulu tales in the person of Uthlakanyana, who speaks before he is born, cheats every one, even his own mother, and shows himself "the best

man in the village" when he is only a babe.
Says his father, "He's best man who first gets
hold of this leg of beef that I throw into the
kraal." So all the rest crowded to the entrance,
and pushed so that none could get it. But
Uthlakanyana crept in underneath at the far
end, and got the beef without any trouble.
Later on he is captured by cannibals, and he
treats them just as trolls and giants are served
in Norse and Celtic tales. They go out one
day while he is fattening, leaving no one with
him but the old mother. "Just untie me,"
says he, "and let us play at boiling one
another." She agrees. "Begin with me; but
mind you take me out soon, for it's only play."

The water is only lukewarm, and the cannibal's mother keeps her word, so he gets out
unhurt, and builds up a roaring fire, telling the
silly woman it will be all the more fun if the
water's dancing about. So he pops her in
and holds down the lid. "Let me out!" she
screams. "It's burning me dreadfully; it's
only fun, you know." "No; you can't be
done, or you would not be able to make that
noise;" so he boils her till she says no more.
Then he puts on her clothes, and lies down in
the old woman's corner. When the children
come in they begin to eat. "This looks just
like mother's hand," says one. "No," says
another; "how can that be? There's mother
on the bed." But Uthlakanyana thinks it best
to be off; so, disguising his voice, he bids them
leave the doorway clear and hobbles out. Just

as he rushes off they fish up their mother's head, and start in pursuit. He is brought up by a wide river; so he turns himself into a weeding-stick. The cannibals trace his footsteps to the brink. "Yes," says one, "he must have got across just here," flinging over the stick to emphasize his words. Safe on the other bank, Uthlakanyana resumes his shape, and thanks them for putting him across. "We thought you were a weeding-stick," replied the discomfited cannibals. But Uthlakanyana is now very hungry: so, meeting a hare, he says, "Stop, master, I've got such a pretty story to tell you." "I'm sure I don't want to hear it," says puss. "Ah, but if you were to hear the beginning of it, you'd not be able to help listening." "Yes, I should, though," persists the hare. "Do you know it's all about those horrid cannibals; they had me cooped up, but I managed to boil their —" And as the hare, in spite of himself, is stopping to listen, our hero gets hold of him, eats him, and makes a flute of one of his leg-bones.

The Zulus have another legend of Uthlakanyana. He lived with a cannibal, with whom he had a quarrel, and resolving to make away with him, he hit on the following expedient. He said one day: "Uncle, let us build a house; then we shall live comfortably and eat our cattle." The cannibal replied, "You are right, child of my sister: let us build a house, for we shall get wet." When the time came to thatch the hut, Uthlakanyana said to the cannibal,

"You go on the top, and I will go inside and pull the thatching needle for you." The cannibal did so. His hair being very long, Uthlakanyana contrives to knot it into the thatch, fastening it so that the poor cannibal could not extricate himself, and there he died, leaving Uthlakanyana to eat in peace.

The Zulus have their riddles, of which the following are specimens:[1]

1. "Guess a man who does not lie down; even when it is morning, he is standing, not having lain down."

Answer. "A pillar, for it does not lie down. If the pillar lies down, the house may fall. Do you not see that the pillar is a man, since it upholds so great a house as this? But it does not fall."

2. "Guess ye a man who does not move, although the wind blows furiously; he just stands erect. The wind throws down trees and houses, and much injury is done, but he is just as if the sky were perfectly calm, and does not move in the least."

Answer. "The ear. Who ever saw the ear of a man move, or being moved by the wind? We see trees and grass and houses move, but not the ear. The man truly moves; if he is carried away by the wind, the ear is not carried away, or, if he falls, it still stands erect, or, if he runs away, it remains the same."

3. "Guess ye some men who are walking, being ten in number. If there is one over the

[1] Callaway's Nursery Tales.

ten, these ten men do not go. They say, 'We cannot go, for here is a prodigy.' These men wonder exceedingly; they are slow in settling the dispute, saying, 'How is it that our number is over ten?' They have no love for the one over the ten."

Answer. "The fingers. Their proper number is only ten. They are matched, going in pairs. Therefore if there is a supernumerary finger, they are no longer fit to go together in pairs or to count with; their counting is bad; there is no agreement, but only difference. This is what we mean when we say they are slow in settling the dispute; that is, if it could be done without pain — the supernumerary finger could be taken off with a word, and thus truly it would be said, 'Away with you! You are not fit for this place.'"

The preceding, chiefly taken from Dr. Callaway's "Nursery Tales, Traditions, and Histories of the Zulus," are sufficient, I trust, to show that the people have a traditional lore which throws light on their history and character.

CHAPTER XXVI.

DECEASED MISSIONARIES OF THE A. B. C. F. M.

IN the first part of this volume sketches were given of three of that heroic band of missionaries, twelve in number, who left this country for South Africa, December 3, 1834. At Cape Town, Messrs. Venable, Lindley, and Dr. Wilson, with their wives, separated from the others and undertook the perilous enterprise of establishing a mission among the Matabele Zulus, who lived far inland. War between the Dutch and natives soon put an end to their work, and, after burying one of their number, Mrs. Wilson, they joined the mission in Zululand. The prospects being dark, Dr. Wilson and Mr. Venable and wife returned home. Rev. George Champion, a colaborer of Mr. Grout and Dr. Adams, held on till his wife's health obliged him to leave. He was expecting to return, but the Lord determined otherwise. At the early age of thirty-one he died at Santa Cruz, one of the Danish West India Islands, December 17, 1841. All who knew him recall his sweet disposition, scholarly ability, and liberality. Having inherited property, he went to Africa and labored there at his own expense, showing throughout an earnest missionary spirit. The savor of his self-denial and consecration has not been lost.

There comes fresh before my memory the form of a dear brother, who was the first American missionary to be buried in South African soil, the Rev. James Bryant. He joined the mission in 1846, but died of pulmonary consumption in 1850. One well observed in regard to him, " He was a man whose life in Africa, though short, emphatically answered life's great end." He possessed in an uncommon degree those qualities that make a faultless missionary. Mr. Bryant's early history is peculiar. His parents, too poor to support all the members of their large family, committed James to the care of a pious colored man named Cato, who resided in Goffstown, N. H. Cato and his wife took the lonely lad to their humble dwelling, and to their hearts. Mrs. Cato, in giving her reminiscences of young Bryant, said, " Oh, he was like a minister. If any of the boys used bad language in his presence, or conducted improperly, he was sure to reprove them." After his conversion he was assisted by some friends to prepare for college. Graduating from Amherst, "a good scholar and ripe Christian," he went to Andover Theological Seminary. For a time he was settled in Littleton, Mass.; but when the call for men to go to Africa reached him he at once responded. Probably his love for the black race, and a desire to pay the debt of gratitude he owed, led him to choose the African field. He quickly mastered the language; translated parts of the Bible, and composed some beautiful hymns. All his works, even to his neat and clear chirography, had a finished look. His brief period of service yielded richer results than are given to many, for before his death he had the joy of seeing a church gathered through his instrumentality. His mind was clear to the last. Mr. Lindley, at whose house he expired, expressed the feelings of his brethren and sisters when he said: "We loved him exceedingly, and had it been possible for others to bear the pain of his sickness, we should all have wished to endure a part. At our next meeting when he shall be spoken of, we shall weep together, as good brothers of the same family weep together for the loss of the best brother they had. And why not? He never spoke to us or thought of us otherwise than in love."

In Rev. Samuel Marsh we all felt that we had a genial, loving, and helpful friend. Located at Itafamasi, he labored for six years, and not without encouragement. Then he was stricken with disease. Though his sufferings were intense, he never lost his faith in God or uttered a word of complaint. After a paroxysm of pain, he once asked: "Why do I linger here?" And when told it seemed to be God's will that he should glorify him by suffering, he remarked, "Oh, yes, it is all right.

Heavenly Father, thy will be done." Allusion having been made to his wife and child, he said, " I have no concern for them ; the Lord can take better care of them than I can." Once, I remember, he clasped his hands and prayed most earnestly that God would make him grateful for the kind friends who were caring for him in his sickness and that he might be patient and submissive under all his sufferings. He delighted to have me read him a book on " Consolation," by Dr. J. W. Alexander. As he approached the dark valley his faith grew stronger and stronger. Then I asked him what was his trust, and he immediately responded, "*The finished work of Christ.*" His end was calm and peaceful. Without a struggle his soul passed into the arms of his Saviour. The " Good Pilot," as he called the Lord Jesus just before his departure, conducted him safely into the harbor.

His remains lie at the station he founded, and on the hill where he loved to call together the heathen and tell the story of redeeming love.

Mr. Lindley, who saw more of him than most of his brethren, observed : " During all the time he was in health, and in sickness, he never said, or did, or left undone a single thing which tended even in the least degree to weaken the conviction deep in the minds of all who knew him that he was eminently a man of God. In his family he ever appeared as a beautiful model of a husband and father. . . . He was true and faithful and loving and generous in all the relations and duties of life. It was with an emphasis that we called him 'brother,' so much was he loved by us all."

One whose influence will long be felt among the Zulus was Rev. Silas McKinny, who went to Natal in 1847. Readily mastering the language, he saw much good accomplished at his station, Amahlongwa, but health failed and he came home. He preached in various places in this country with acceptance, and died at Auburn, N. Y., April 21, 1888. It was well said of him, "He was a tender, loving parent, a faithful Christian, and a devoted and self-forgetful minister of the gospel."

Two years before he left Natal, his wife, Fanny Nelson McKinny, "slept in Jesus," and was buried in the little cemetery at Adams. Although of a timid, shrinking disposition, her calm, good judgment and earnest faithfulness as a Christian wife and mother endeared her to all who knew her. It may be said of her, "She hath done what she could."

Another beloved missionary, Rev. William Ireland, born in England, but educated in this country, died in Boston, Mass., October 12, 1888, after forty years of service.

Leaving his wife in Africa, he came home to rest, visit his children, and then resume his labors. But the Lord said, "Come up higher." He spent the first thirteen years of his useful mission life at Ifumi. He was then requested to take charge of the training institution at Adams, a work for which he had exceptional qualifications. Through his instrumentality that school gradually rose to great importance. Mr. Ireland was for many years treasurer of the Zulu Mission, and was so correct and so good a penman that his books will compare favorably with those of the best mercantile establishments. He was methodical, conscientious, kind, and sympathetic, an affectionate husband and father, gentlemanly in his manners, a safe counselor, and, above all, spiritually minded and earnestly devoted to mission work. He was married twice : first, to Jane Wilson, of New Ipswich, Mass., who died at Ifumi, January 25, 1862. His second wife was Oriana Grout, daughter of Rev. Aldin Grout, the missionary. She still remains in the field.

The reader will remember that when Mr. Wilder and myself, with our wives, sailed for Natal, we were accompanied by Rev. and Mrs. Andrew Abraham. They were located in a distant part of Natal among wild heathen, and there they remained till death. Mr. Abraham was not unworthy of the name, "Father of the faithful." His faith never wavered, though he toiled long without seeing results. When a brighter day dawned, and he beheld the heathen emerging from barbarism, and building houses in European style, his faith rose wonderfully. He said to me one day, as we were riding over the mission reserve, "Brother Tyler, I expect to see most of these hills covered with the abodes of Christian natives." He was permitted to see a goodly number of them thus covered. Nothing seemed to discourage him. One day he was cementing a cistern, and came out just in time to see his house enveloped in flames. Ten minutes later, his chapel also was consumed. Although minus hat, boots, and coat, he did not despair, but began immediately to build anew, nor did he stop till he had a more substantial dwelling. His death in the night of September 13, 1878, was very sudden, and probably due to heart disease, as he appeared in usual health the day previous. He was considered our best translator, and to him the mission had committed the work of preparing the Old Testament for the press. The grief of not only his associates, but of all the natives who knew him, was profound when told of his death. A chief remarked, "Our teacher was a good man and did good to all."

Mrs. Abraham lived but a short time after her husband's decease. The shock she received may have hastened her own departure. That she was his true helper in mission work the native women at Mapumulo as well as all who knew her can testify.

A more genial and humorous companion, a missionary with a more practical turn of mind than Rev. H. A. Wilder is rarely found in a foreign field; as one said of him, he had a "many-sided capacity." He was so absorbed in plans to advance the natives in civilization, as well as Christianity, he probably overworked himself. In taking a long journey to select a site for a new station, he had a severe attack of illness, from which he never fully recovered. He died in Hartford, Conn., September 7, 1877. His son, Rev. George Wilder, occupies the station made vacant by the death of his father. Mrs. Wilder is now in this country.

Rev. Seth B. Stone began his work at the Ifafa station in 1850. Faithful as a preacher, busily employed in translating parts of the Bible, composing hymns, teaching and discharging other missionary duties, he continued in the field till the ill health of his wife necessitated his return to America. His heart was in Africa, and to the last his prayers were for the good of the Zulus. His death occurred in New York City, January 27, 1877. His widow is still living.

Joining the mission in 1862, Rev. Charles H. Lloyd entered on his work with a spirit of earnest consecration. Battling with disease, he was ever patient and showed true Christian submission. He lived only two years, dying at the Umvoti Mission station, in 1865. Mr. Grout wrote of him: "When the shortness of his missionary life was referred to, he said, 'Yes, I would have had it otherwise; but I have not a doubt that God called me here, and I am glad I came. If God cuts my life thus short, I can only say, Thy will be done.'" At his request, he was buried near a large tree in front of the native church, that the people might be reminded of one who had it in his heart to preach to them the gospel.

Mr. Lloyd was an accomplished gentleman,

a fine musician, with a large share of practical common sense, was quick to read character and anxious to know the best methods of doing good. Had he lived, he would doubtless have proved an efficient and successful missionary. His death-bed testimony of the power of religion to sustain and comfort the soul will never be forgotten by the natives on the Umvoti station.

Mrs. Catharine C. Lloyd, daughter of the distinguished physician, Dr. Willard Parker, of New York City, remained in Natal after the death of her husband, working with enthusiasm and success, until 1870. She then married Dr. Newton Lindley, son of the missionary, Rev. Daniel Lindley, and returned soon after to this country. She died in New York, July 23, 1879.

We cannot speak too highly of this self-denying and laborious missionary. Thoroughly educated, in possession of all that wealth could furnish, she left her refined home and labored earnestly and untiringly for the degraded Zulus. Great was her joy when she was permitted to see a large number of them emancipated from ignorance and superstition through her efforts. While in the field, she wrote letters home which awakened deep interest, and which were collected in a volume entitled "The Seeds and the Sheaves," published by Randolph & Co.

Rev. Elijah Robbins began mission work in 1851 at Umzumbe, where he remained thirteen years. He then established a theological school at Adams, the success of which is in a great measure the fruit of his zeal and perseverance. Native preachers, now in various parts of the field, are ready to testify to the diligence and thoroughness of their teacher. He died July 1, 1889, joining his wife in the "better land." Mrs. Robbins had died only a few months previously. Testimonies of the worth of Mrs. Addie Bissell Robbins are impressive and tender. One is from the pen of Rev. Charles Kilbon, who knew her well: "A precious wife and mother has gone from the home which she lighted by her smile and animated and inspired by her buoyant and energetic nature. A beloved companion in work has been taken from our mission circle. A vigorous worker for the good of this people has forever ceased from her labors. How she used, with her light and agile form, in days of health, to flit from house to house over the station, leaving words of instruction, of warning, of comfort, as needed! She has gone to a higher sphere of activity, where she will never tire."

Mrs. Holbrook, of Mapumulo, wrote: "She was a rare woman, beloved by natives and whites alike. An enthusiastic missionary, a consecrated Christian, devoted to her family, her people, and her God."

Rev. David Rood, who died in Covert, Mich., April 8, 1891, entered the field in 1847, together with Rev. Samuel Marsh.

After forty years of faithful service he came to this country to rest, but did not wholly abandon the hope of a return to Africa till a short time before his death. He wrote to me repeatedly, saying, "My heart is there." Rev. Lewis Grout, one of his early associates, truthfully says of him: "He was gentle, quiet, modest, winning in his ways, yet strong, courageous, earnest, confident in his work, assured that it was God who would make it to prosper and prevail."

As I remarked in the first part of this volume, it was through Mr. Rood's instrumentality that I was led to choose Natal as my field of labor. Soon after reaching that colony, my wife and I paid Mr. and Mrs. Rood a visit. Their station was far removed from the abodes of white men, and their surroundings were what most people would call gloomy in the extreme. But those devoted missionaries seemed to be in the enjoyment of genuine happiness. Their hearty and sincere welcome to a participation in their joys nerved us for our future labors.

Our lamented brother early acquired a knowledge of the Zulu dialect, and was able to preach in it far more easily than he could in English. He threw his whole soul into the work and thoroughly enjoyed it. He occupied various important posts, but his greatest work was at the Umvoti station. While chairman of the mission, he manifested wisdom, decision, and a tender regard for the feelings of his brethren. In translating the Scriptures and preparing elementary books for our schools, he was thorough and skillful; but he excelled as a preacher and spiritual adviser. His last conversation was about Jesus Christ, the "Rock" on which he had built his faith and hope, and his last words were, "I am going home." When unable to speak, a pleasant smile on his countenance was a response to a brother's inquiry. He died as he had lived, a true Christian man, one who had no occasion for fears or sighs or regrets. He left the wife of his youth and sharer of his toils, and his two children, with the sweet consciousness that heaven was his home. He has joined the sainted Adams, Lindley, Bryant, Marsh, and other fellow-toilers in the African vineyard, and Zulus also, saved through his instrumentality. I think of him as beckoning to the old soldiers who fought by his side for King Immanuel on Afric's dark coast to join him in the better land, where they can recount battles fought and victories won.

Rev. Jacob L. Döhne, a German, who was for several years connected with the mission, died in 1879. He was a fine linguist, and prepared an elaborate dictionary of the Zulu language containing over 10,000 words. Of this work a competent judge remarked: "It is not only the first dictionary of a South African tongue that can claim any approximation to completeness, but is also a living monument to the author's industry, careful observation, and unfaltering perseverance."

The mother of Rev. Myron Winslow Pinkerton died when her son was three years old, but when she gave him the above name, she said, "I hope he will be a missionary." While in college Mr. Pinkerton said that the wish of his mother, which had been made known to him as soon as he could comprehend it, would often come to his mind. Later, when the time came for him to choose his field, he observed, "Perhaps there will be men who would wish to go to Turkey and Japan, while few will go to Africa."

The station he occupied at first was Umtwalume, in company with Mr. Wilder; but in 1875 he moved to a place called Induduma, more than a hundred miles from any of his brethren. There he toiled until the inquiry arose, "Who will explore Umzila's country with reference to sending men there?"

Well do I remember his appearance and his words when his brethren said to him, "It is our unanimous opinion that *you* are the man." "You place," he observed, "a solemn and fearful responsibility on me; but if it is God's will, I will not shrink from it." He took his wife and children to America, because, as he remarked, of the possibility of his being removed by death, while away.

I might particularize with regard to the hopefulness and courage with which he met obstacle after obstacle in his attempts to start on that long and perilous journey. In the inscrutable providence of God, he was smitten with malarial fever and died while on the way,

Mrs. Susan W. Tyler.

November 10, 1880. He was buried under a large, moss-covered tree, on the banks of the Gabula River, a native Christian reading the funeral service.

A nobler, more enthusiastic and self-reliant missionary than Mr. Pinkerton it would be difficult to find. Why he was so suddenly cut down in the strength of manhood and midst of usefulness we cannot tell. The Lord will doubtless reveal to us the reason in another world.

Mrs. Pinkerton now resides in Chicago, Ill.

Mr. John A. Butler, whose narrow escape from a crocodile has already been mentioned, responded to a call for a missionary printer, and went to Natal in 1850. His health was so weakened by the terrible ordeal through which he had passed that he was forced soon to return to America. Though never again robust, his life was greatly prolonged by the unwearied care of his wife. He died August 27, 1889, leaving a widow and two children.

Of her who was the companion of my joys and sorrows, the light of my dwelling, the devoted wife, mother, and missionary, I must leave others to speak. A brother with whom we had been associated from the first, one who soon followed her to the heavenly world, Mr. Ireland, wrote as follows : " Becoming a Christian in early life, Mrs. Tyler gave herself to missionary work with all her heart and soul, and during all these years has impressed those who had the privilege of knowing her, as one who possessed an unusually faultless character, and whose life was filled with Christian consecration. Her interest in the Zulus was ever finding ways to manifest itself in their behalf, especially in her judicious advice to them when in trouble. Hence we are not surprised that large numbers of them, both Christians and heathen, learned implicitly to trust and love her, oftentimes better than their own kindred. . . . As long as she was able to converse, her room was the center of peacefulness, brightness, and joy, and she begged to have no sorrow or gloom felt, or tears shed, as she was simply 'going home.' Her earnest words of appeal to the natives who entered her sick room, or, when too weak to speak, her bright smile and peaceful face, were powerful influences for good. At the funeral service it was truthfully said, ' The grave has not closed in Natal over one who led a purer, gentler, and more useful life.' " Mrs. Pixley, a missionary, wrote as follows : —

"A large company of both Christian and heathen natives gathered at the burial, coming from a distance in the surrounding region, and from her old Esidumbini station. It was pathetic to see one old heathen man, the day after the funeral, come weeping that he had not received word in time for him to take a last look at his dear teacher's face, and mourn with others at her burial. . . . During the last weeks of her illness, she had such a sweet assurance because of her perfect trust in Christ, that peace, perfect peace, was her motto. She loved to talk of Christ and his nearness, and spoke much of Bible study. Her room was cheery, bright, and the center of joy and peace. While we mourn the loss of such a friend and fellow-worker, we rejoice in her bright example, praying that her mantle may fall upon us with a double portion of the spirit which characterized her, and that the seed sown by her, in prayer and labor for the people, may grow into an abundant harvest. . . . In her long missionary life she was permitted to see many spiritual children, and many, we doubt not, were waiting for her at the gate of the City, as she entered in."

A friend in this country wrote of her: —

"Those who knew Mrs. Tyler could not fail to recognize her as one who had so trained herself that all Christian dispositions, a tranquil nature, a loving spirit, meekness, gentleness, disinterestedness, had become so habitual as to be unconscious to herself. And yet, with this measure of quiet grace, she was eminent in active labors. She 'labored much in the Lord.'

"It has been said, 'The best work given to any missionary is the ordering of a Christian home in a heathen land.' This, in connection with her work for the heathen, Mrs. Tyler perfectly fulfilled. The home over which she presided so brightly and usefully was characterized by the grace and cheer and restfulness of the home which Jesus loved at Bethany.

"She spent her life in cultivating the ideal and practical side of character among the Zulus, heathen and Christian, showing by her own example the value of a life that blends spiritual truth and care-taking, home-making duties in one rounded whole."

On the seventeenth of November, 1887, she fell asleep and awakened to be "forever with the Lord."

CHAPTER XXVII.

NATIVE EDUCATION.

NATIVE education is receiving more attention than ever, not only from American, but other societies. Our hope for the future regeneration of Africa lies in the young. Consequently, training institutions for youth of both sexes, at central points, are deemed a necessity. They are not designed to take the place of primary schools, but to advance pupils to a higher stage.

Of these institutions, the Amanzimtote Seminary at Adams is at present the only training school for Zulu lads connected with the American mission. This was commenced in 1865, by Rev. William Ireland. The medium of instruction is the English language, which pupils must understand to a certain degree before entrance. Connected with the seminary is an industrial department, in which are taught carpentering, blacksmithing, shoemaking, and printing. The great object in view is to give practical training. Its religious character is of a high order, the teachers aiming first of all at moral regeneration, without which their training may prove a curse instead of a blessing. Stress is laid upon Bible study, and the importance of overcoming hereditary prejudices and superstitions. Its record thus far is a noble one. Most of its graduates are useful members of society, some of them being teachers and preachers.

Jubilee Hall was opened in December, 1885, at the semi-centennial anniversary of the mission. It is a large, commodious structure, accommodating about one hundred pupils, and costing $15,000, a part of which was contributed by American friends and the remainder by Natal colonists. Beautifully located on a grassy hill sloping towards the river Amanzimtote (*sweet water*), it commands a fine view of the Indian Ocean, eight miles distant. Here the students find a true *home*.

Those interested in this institution hope much for its future. If funds are forthcoming, a medical department is to be opened at Adams, and the boys will receive such instruction as will overcome much of their superstitious fear of disease. In every department there is opportunity for enlargement, and to no more worthy object can assistance be rendered.

The theological school was commenced in 1869 by Rev. Elijah Robbins. From time to time men have gone forth to be missionaries to their own people. We trust many more will avail themselves of the faithful teaching and preparation for service which is given them by Rev. Charles Kilbon, who has charge of that department.

The Inanda Seminary for girls is not only a school, but a home. From sixty to seventy

bright girls, varying in age from twelve to sixteen, most of them born of Christian parents, are here taught the elements of a good education. The success of the school is owing in a great measure to the wise judgment and unwearied efforts of Mrs. Edwards, who began it in 1869.

The course of study pursued embraces biblical history, harmony of the Gospels, reading, translation and dictation in Zulu and English, writing, arithmetic, geography, history, physiology, and English composition. Special attention is paid to needlework in its various branches, as well as domestic employment and gardening. The fee for board and tuition is twenty-five dollars per annum for each pupil. So anxious are girls to attend this school that they frequently run away from their kraals, pursued by their fathers or brothers, whose chief desire is to secure the cattle for which they may be sold when of a marriageable age. After a palaver of half an hour or so, if they find the girl is determined to stop, they leave her and go home. The girls cultivate twenty acres of land and endeavor to make the school self-supporting. This end has not yet been wholly accomplished. Friends in America have kindly assumed the responsibility of supporting some whose parents are too poor, or unwilling to furnish the means.

The girls are taught singing and render difficult music by note correctly and sweetly, taking the soprano and alto with ease in anthems, duets, etc. Their new building, Edwards Hall, erected by gifts from mission circles in this country, amounting to $5,000, is all that can be desired for convenience and utility. In describing an examination at Inanda, a few years ago, Mrs. Tyler wrote: —

"As I sat on the platform facing forty girls, two at each desk, I wondered what would be the future of them all, and I am thankful that my faith, which has been many times weakened by disappointments, did not fail to predict a happy life for them. They have stepped a long way out of heathenism, and, in their recitations and conversation, appear to me to know better than ever what the 'Light' means, and what an infinite blessing has come to them through Christian teaching. It is a great gain to secure them for several years, so that their habits may become fixed and their minds have elevating influences which they do not find at their homes. I counted ten whose mothers had lived with me when they were children."

Umzumbe Home is another school for girls, but, unlike Inanda Seminary, the majority of scholars come from heathen kraals, without previous preparation. Of the Christian influence exerted and faithful instruction given, too much cannot be said. Graduates of this school, after four years' study (many of them having become Christians), exert a most salutary influence in their heathen homes. The good they may do cannot be estimated. The enlarged accommodations provide for sixty girls, but there is room for substantial aid in various departments, which would be money well invested. The course of study pursued is similar to that of Inanda, out-of-door employment included.

In addition to those already referred to, and the daily schools at each station, there are the kraal schools, so called on account of their being within the native villages, and at some distance from the mission stations. Formerly native chiefs refused to have their children educated. A change has come over them. They now say, "We are too old to learn, but our children are not; send us teachers." In some cases they are willing to assist in erecting a schoolhouse, and to assume the responsibility, in part, of paying the teacher. An instance has lately occurred of a chief's making a law that all the children of his tribe shall be taught, the fathers to be fined ten shillings each if they refuse to send their offspring to the school, and a child one shilling if absent purposely. It is pleasant to see a well-made and convenient building with doors and windows, provided with benches, slates, blackboards, and other essentials, by the side of a kraal in a locality far away from any missionary. The children, it is true, learn under difficulties. Girls whose business it is to take care of babies bring them in leather sacks, slung on their shoulders. Herd boys drive their flocks of goats and cattle to a hill opposite the school, where they can watch them and study at the same time. The teachers are usually graduates of the seminaries, some of whom conduct services on the Sabbath. When fairly started with twenty-five pupils, a little aid is afforded by the Natal government. All these schools are under the supervision of missionaries, and the truth made known in them has frequently been blessed to the conversion of souls.

The efforts of all missionary bodies for the education of the Natal Zulus have invariably met with sympathy from the English authorities. Officials have declared that mission work in isolated parts of the colony has helped materially in the government of the natives. Not only in many instances are mission reserves laid out of the native locations, each one including six thousand or more acres, but grants from an educational fund are made to station schools. Doubtless one reason why the government has indorsed the labors of missionaries is the fact that as much as possible they have abstained from entering the arena of politics, rigidly adhering to their own appropriate work. Mr. Robert Plant, inspector of native education, a man eminently adapted for his post, has proposed to the Educational Council a scheme which seems wise and feasible. It provides for the establishment of small industrial schools in the more thickly populated parts of the native locations, each to supply the needs of two hundred and fifty children with one European and five native teachers. The expenditure for this

PUPILS OF THE INANDA SEMINARY.

enterprise he estimates at £8,000, and regular instruction will be provided for six thousand children.

It is evident that European merchants in Natal are the gainers as educational and Christian work progresses among the natives. Rev. James Dalzell, M.D., a scholarly and able Scotch missionary, who reported at a late missionary conference that he had seen, in two years, his native adherents multiplied a hundredfold, computed that while a native kraal required only £2 worth of imported goods, each mission native required £20. Reckoning the Zulu church members in the colony at four thousand, their commercial requirements aggregate £80,000 per annum. So much in a pecuniary point of view are the Natal colonists indebted to Christian missions.

The publications of the American Mission in the Zulu language, from the beginning to the present time, are: the Bible entire, dictionaries, grammars, histories (one ecclesiastical), hymn books, arithmetics, geographies, primers, catechisms, a monthly newspaper, — The Morning Star, — and a variety of tracts. Other societies have published books for their schools and stations, but none to such an extent as the American. The Zulu Bible, printed by the American Bible Society, answers not only for missionaries of the American Board of Commissioners for Foreign Missions, but for Norwegian, German, and Swedish societies, as well as the London Missionary Society among the Matabele Zulus.

CHAPTER XXVIII.

THE MISSIONARY OUTLOOK.

IN 1885 was celebrated the "Jubilee," or semi-centennial anniversary of the American Zulu Mission. With one exception, the pioneers had gone to their reward. There were, however, some veteran laborers to mingle with their younger brethren in the festivities of the occasion. Jubilee Hall was then opened by the governor of the colony, who, together with leading colonists, expressed hearty sympathy and interest. Rev. William Ireland read a history of the mission's five decades, showing a steady advance from the beginning.

Statistics from the mission at the close of 1889 show that there were sixteen churches, with a membership of eleven hundred and fifty-five; under Sabbath-school instruction, fourteen hundred and eighty; missionaries, thirty-eight; native helpers, including teachers and preachers, one hundred and sixty-seven; money contributed for church work, education, and charitable purposes, during the year, over one thousand dollars.

The East Central African Mission, a branch of the one in Natal, was commenced by Rev. W. Wilcox and wife in 1883. Its prospects for a time were very encouraging. Messrs.

Richards, Ousley, Bates, and their wives went to that field; the languages were mastered, parts of the Bible printed, and everything went on prosperously. But Mr. Wilcox left the work and Messrs. Richards and Bates, on account of fever, were obliged to leave. The latter has joined the Natal Mission. Mr. Richards came to the United States and retired from the service of the Board. Mr. Ousley followed him, owing to serious illness, but hopes to return shortly. This brother was a slave, born on the plantation of Mr. Joseph Davis, brother of Jefferson Davis, president of the Confederate States. He was freed at the time the slaves were emancipated by order of President Lincoln. After studying at Fisk University and Oberlin, he received appointment to the East Central African Mission, whither he went with his wife, who is also a graduate of Fisk University. These are the first colored missionaries sent by the American Board of Commissioners for Foreign Missions to Southern Africa. Mr. Ousley believes that the colored men from our southern states can endure the malarial climate of Africa better than white men. Neither he nor his wife has suffered from fever as much in Africa as they did in this country. Miss Jones, a colored lady who went out to assist the Ousleys, does not complain of the climate. If it is true that our colored brethren and sisters can labor in those malarial districts without succumbing as do white missionaries, how important that they be sent there! Few more inviting fields are to be found in the Dark Continent than this.

The force in the field at the present writing is represented by Rev. John B. Bennet and wife and Miss Jones; Rev. Mr. Bunker and wife are, however, designated to it, and sailed in February, 1890. Rev. Mr. Wilcox and wife also returned in the same month.

In the foregoing pages, the work of the *American Zulu Mission* has been chiefly considered. Let no one think that I am disposed to underrate the labors of other evangelical bodies. Noble men and women of various sections of the Christian Church are toiling faithfully for the good of the natives, and, so far as I have observed, most harmoniously. There is no clashing out there. If there is any rivalry, it is that of brave soldiers, ambitious to advance the glory of their heavenly King. One should visit a foreign mission field to see illustrated the remark Dr. Livingstone once made: "All classes of Christians find that sectarian rancor soon dies out when they are working together among and for the real heathen."

The Dutch in Natal have what is called a Boer Farm Mission, of an interesting character. One of the results of a late revival of religion among the farmers was an earnest desire to Christianize the natives living on their farms, and it is pleasant to behold school-houses, places of worship, and other proofs of evangelistic enterprise in a field hitherto neglected.

English Wesleyan Methodists, and Scotch Presbyterians of the Free Church, confine their labors principally to Natal, while the Germans (Berlin and Hanoverian), Norwegians, Swedes, and missionaries of the Church of England have stations in Cape Colony and in Zululand. Since the latter country has come under British jurisdiction, happier results from missionary efforts may be expected than while it was under the reign of despotism.

Until quite recently, non-Protestant societies have not made any strenuous effort to convert the Zulus. There is, however, now in the field an order of Benedictine monks, called Trappists, who are manifesting extraordinary zeal. Their chief monastery, Marianhill, is a few miles from the seaport. The abbot, Francis Pfaner, a German, who superintends the establishment, is a gentleman of great shrewdness and intelligence. When I visited the place he took me about, and willingly explained his plans and methods of labor. Evidently, in his opinion, civilization is the primary step to be taken in elevating the heathen. There were on the ground one hundred and seventy monks and one hundred and twenty nuns; more were expected. Three hundred native boys and girls were under instruction, chiefly industrial. Twenty thousand acres of land have been purchased, a large part of which is under cultivation. All the workshops were full of activity, but I noticed that the men did not utter a word. Perpetual silence, it appears, is imposed on all monks under the Benedictine rule. To an Englishman who asked the abbot the reason for this, the reply was: "There are reasons spiritual and secular. Silence is spiritually beneficial. It is secularly beneficial, inasmuch as there is no quarreling when there is no talking, and there is much more work done." Zulu lads, however. chatted and laughed *ad libitum.* They would not have been Zulus otherwise.

Various industries engage the Trappists, among which is bee culture. Newspapers in Polish, German, English, and Zulu are published at the monastery. Pains are taken to extend their influence among the natives. A brass band consisting of thirty sandaled monks marches occasionally through the streets of the nearest town, playing as they go, and are followed by Zulus clothed in dark fustian with polished helmets on their heads.

To what this extraordinary Trappist movement will grow, it is impossible to predict.

I trust it will appear from what has been said that the outlook, so far at least as the American Zulu Mission is concerned, is calculated to cheer, rather than to depress. News from the field clearly indicates an advance all along the line. Societies of Christian Endeavor are springing up; the cause of temperance is gaining ground; schools are well attended; Sabbath audiences are growing larger; "spirit doctors" are losing their hold of the native mind; the axe of the gospel is laid at the root of polygamy and attendant evils;

The Missionary Outlook. 265

Christianity, hand in hand with civilization, is moving on. Is the time far distant when those qualities of valor, obedience, and endurance which the Zulus displayed when in a state of barbarism will be conspicuous in promoting the Redeemer's glory? Has not God in his providence sent his servants to Natal, spared their lives, enabled them to master the native language, translate the Bible and other books, and put in operation the machinery of means, preparatory to carrying the blessings of Christianity into Africa's dark interior? What base of operations could have been selected more suitable for this object? What strategic point could we have laid hold of on the southeastern coast better than this? Recruits from our mission schools will doubtless go as missionaries to the Matabele and other Zulu-speaking tribes. The way was opened last year when Umcitwa and Yona, a man and his wife from the Umzumbe station, joined the mission to the Matabele tribe. On their journey, Umcitwa took a severe cold which resulted in his death soon after reaching his destination. Who can tell, however, what results may follow his example?

Though I have spoken hopefully respecting the Zulu Mission and its importance with reference to the future regeneration of Africa, I am compelled to add, with sorrow, that there are influences at work that will undo much that has been done, and hinder progress, unless God in his mercy interposes. The streams of intemperance and vice flowing into Natal imperil not only the spiritual, but the physical existence of the natives. A large body of Christ's servants are needed at once to counteract those influences. The Zulus are in a transition state. Much will be lost by delay. The remark lately made by Mr. Stanley in reference to the importance of reinforcing Christian missions in Central, will apply equally to South, Africa: "If we want to hold our ground, we must not send little parties of workers, as heretofore, but must pour in men by the scores and even by the fifties."

Death and illness have sadly depleted the number of missionaries. The few left in the field, overburdened, ask with a pathos that should reach the hearts of God's people at home, —

"Do they come, do they come?
We are feeble and worn,
And we are passing like shadows away.
But the harvest is white. Lo, yonder the dawn!
For laborers, for laborers, we pray!"

To those who may inquire, "Are the results of your work among the Zulus commensurate with the toil and money expended?" I reply: If judged by worldly standards, they may not appear so; but truly no serious-minded man will gauge them by figures alone. No tabular view can adequately represent what has been done. Of this we are sure: it is God's work, and it cannot be a failure. One has truthfully said: "God's true missionary goes where He

JOSIAH, TEACHER IN THE BOYS' HIGH SCHOOL AT ADAMS.

sends him, and he succeeds, though all he may do is to plow up the hard ground and gather out the stones to leave a fair field for the sower. And in God's eyes many a man who, by the armful or wagonload, brings sheaves to the garner is only reaping from others' sowing."

If we could point to a single Zulu who has been savingly converted, that alone would prove that our labors have not been in vain. But, thank God! we can adduce instances not a few of self-denial, humility, holy living, resignation to the divine will, heroic faith, and joy in the near prospect of death. I think I am safe in saying that, as a rule, converted Zulus are quite as consistent in their daily life as average church members in Christian lands. It is unreasonable to suppose that, with the few advantages they possess, they should rise speedily to the standard of intelligent piety attained in more highly favored countries.

What Rev. John McKenzie, formerly of the London Missionary Society, has said in regard to Bechuana Christians applies to Zulus: "It is not to be expected that a loquacious, news-telling people, unaccustomed to solitude and to consecutive thought or study, should, on their conversion to Christianity, become at once remarkable for their elevated spirituality and for delighting in protracted seasons of prayer, meditation, and communion with God."

Before closing this chapter, let me ask my readers, especially those who are young, strong, and qualified to engage in mission work, Do you really believe that the gospel is the grand instrument devised by God for the elevation of the degraded? And has the command, "Go, teach all nations," lost any of its force since it was given by the Master? Have you individually and seriously inquired, with a desire to ascertain God's will, "Is it my duty to carry the gospel to the heathen?" Should you do so, would the cause of God in this land suffer from your absence? On the other hand, would not an impetus be given to it, thus illustrating that heavenly law, "There is that scattereth, and yet increaseth"? Go and tell the benighted the story of Jesus and his love, and even they will exclaim in the language of inspiration, "How beautiful are the feet of them that . . . bring glad tidings of good things!" Go, and if successful in your work, you will hear from the lips of converted heathen what you cannot hear if you remain in your native land: "For our sakes you left home and kindred. You were the only almoners of God's bounty to us. You found us naked; you have clothed us. Ignorant, you have taught us. We delighted in war; you have taught us the principles of peace. We were in the depths of degradation; you have raised us to sit together in heavenly places in Christ Jesus. We will never cease to thank God for sending you to tell us of the great salvation." That will pay for all your toil and sacrifices.

CHAPTER XXIX.

FACTS CONCERNING NATAL.

NATAL lies in the same latitude south as New Orleans north; is eight hundred miles from the Cape of Good Hope, and seventy-five hundred miles from England. Mail steamers from London reach it in about twenty-five days, stopping at the Cape, Port Elizabeth, and East London. It has an area of twenty-one thousand two hundred and fifty miles, and a seaboard of one hundred and eighty. Vasco da Gama, a Portuguese navigator, sighted it on Christmas day, five years after Columbus discovered America, and it received its name, *Terra Natalis*, in honor of that day.

The first attempt to colonize it was made in 1823 by a party of Englishmen with Lieutenant Farwell at its head. Chaka, the Zulu king at that time, ceded to them what now comprises the colony. Soon after, the same Zulu potentate made Captain Allen Gardiner, an Englishman, a grant of the same territory, evidently not regarding the previous cession as *bona fide*. The country was once thickly populated, but that despot so devastated it by his armies that only here and there could be found a few stragglers, and they were in a state of starvation.

The first Christian missionaries to Natal were those of the American Board, who landed in 1835. Wars between the natives and Dutch farmers, immigrants from the Cape Colony, and afterwards between the English and Dutch, kept the country in a state of insecurity till 1843, when it was proclaimed a British possession. Soon after, a governor was appointed, and an executive council established. Quiet having been restored, natives, fleeing from tyranny and witchcraft in Zululand, entered in large numbers.

The first object saluting the newcomer to Natal is the lighthouse, a massive, costly structure, situated on a high bluff, visible from a long distance. The coast, lined with thick gnarled bushes, twenty feet or more in height, interspersed with euphorbia, Kaffir boom, and palm trees, presents a pretty appearance. The rivers emptying into the ocean are indicated by the surf as it dashes over the sandbanks at their mouths. Of these, twenty-three in number, only one is navigable, the Umzimkulu, and that but a short distance. Until lately, entrance to the Natal harbor has been choked by sand, and this has proved a serious obstacle to colonial prosperity. At a great expense breakwaters have been constructed, so that ships drawing sixteen feet of water can now enter with safety. Experts in engineering predict that a still greater depth of water will be secured. The harbor, once entered, is all that can be desired — sheltered, commodious, and sufficiently deep. The customhouse and warehouses along the docks, where ships load and unload, remind one of English and American ports. The contrast between 1849 and 1891 is simply marvelous. Telegraphic communication is established, not only throughout Natal, but with the Transvaal, Orange Free State, and various ports along the eastern coast. A submarine cable between Zanzibar and Aden brings the colony into communication with Great Britain. Mail steamers run constantly, the price of first-class passage being not far from two hundred dollars; second-class, one hundred and fifty. There are lines of boats carrying cargo and a limited number of passengers, having excellent accommodations, which make the passage in a longer time and at reduced rates.

Natal has been called by its admirers an "Elysium in South Africa"; and not without reason. Probably England has no brighter gem among her colonies. For beauty of scenery and salubrity of climate she is deservedly distinguished. Perhaps allowance should be made for the writer, who for twenty-three years of his Natal life was not ill a single week, but it is doubtful whether on the globe there is a spot where the atmosphere is clearer and the sky brighter than during the winter months, from May to October. The evenings are then generally free from clouds, and the stars shine with extraordinary brilliancy. In 1858 it was reported that during the six months of winter there were ninety-seven starlit evenings. An English scientist remarked: "The stars seem half as large and half as bright again as they ever do in England, and shine with a steady effulgence." In regard to the moon he added: "In the latitudes of this colony the moon occasionally comes within four times its own breadth of the zenith as it crosses the meridian. At such times the moonshine is often of such intense brilliancy that strong black shadows are cast by it, and the smallest objects can be distinctly seen by its aid."

During the winter there is very little rain; sometimes for two or three months none at all. The thermometer ranges, during that time, from 40° to 60°. Snow falls occasionally in the upper districts, but never on the coast, and rarely is the frost severe enough within fifteen miles of the sea to injure bananas or sweet potato vines. The average temperature for the three hottest and three coldest months, taken from accurate observation is as follows: —

December, January, and February. Highest, 97° 5'; mean, 72° 2'; lowest, 53° 3'.

June, July, and August. Highest 83° 4'; mean, 56° 7'; lowest, 31° 9'.

The colony rises in terraces above the level of the Indian Ocean till it reaches the Drakensberg or "Dragon's Mountains," a high range which has sometimes been called the "Appenines of South Africa." This range divides Natal from the Transvaal and Orange Free State. Some of the peaks are nearly eight thousand feet high, and during the winter months are frequently capped with snow. In summer the heat is as intense as during the dog days of July and August in New England, but the frequent thunderstorms are invariably followed by cool days and nights. In regard to these storms, Dr. Robert Mann observed: " They must be seen before a notion of their character can be realized. Sometimes the end of a great storm cloud looms from the horizon with a splendid glow or brush of light bursting from behind it at each discharge, and throwing the black masses forward in strong relief. At other times the foldings of the troubled and twisted clouds are rendered conspicuous by colored lines and sheets of fire, which exceed in complication and variety of device the most ingenious display of pyrotechny. As many as fifty-six distinct lightning flashes in every minute may sometimes be counted, rising in this way from one spot of the horizon; and the exhibition may be seen continuing on the same scale for one or two hours at a time."

Tornadoes seldom occur. The only one I remember was in 1850, which stripped the native huts of their grass covering and tore up trees by the roots, but soon spent itself without causing loss of life. Natalians have a way of guarding against sunstroke which Americans might imitate; they wear cork helmets, well ventilated and covered with white.

The vital statistics of the colony show a record of mortality said to be low, compared with other countries. Persons troubled with pulmonary complaints often derive substantial aid, if they reach South Africa before the disease has become too deeply seated. Those who have adopted Natal as their home are generally contented with their lot. At first some of them had to "rough it," but persistent industry rewarded many with the luxuries as well as the comforts of life. I recall what was designated as the "pumpkin and *mealie* (corn) dispensation" of 1850. A number of immigrants, shipwrecked as they were crossing the Natal sandbar, were for a time reduced to straits, obliged to subsist on Indian corn and pumpkins; but they endured their trials bravely and cheerfully, and now, being well off, can remind their children, when they are disposed to complain, of what their parents had to contend with in those early colonial days. One competent to speak from experience has observed: —

"Natal is not a country in which to realize a fortune. By steady work a man beginning with even a small capital may rapidly acquire a competence and a comfortable home. From a social point of view Natal is altogether delightful. A man who does not crave millions, but happiness, may assuredly find the latter."

In 1889, on account of the rapidly developing gold fields and rush to South Africa, the demand for skilled labor was great. Artisans, masons, carpenters, miners then obtained high wages. The times have changed somewhat, but physicians, printers, lawyers, clerks, and bookkeepers are now well remunerated.

The cost of living, though greater than it was formerly, is not beyond the means of the majority. Good beef, mutton, and bacon can be had at twelve and one-half cents per pound. Fish, at the seaport, is cheap and abundant. Fowls are twenty-five cents apiece. Oysters can be had by knocking them off the rocks at low tide; they are small, but of good flavor. Game is sometimes obtainable in the market, and vegetables of various kinds are abundant. Fruit is plentiful and cheap. Bananas, pineapples, mangoes, oranges, mandarins, limes, peaches, lemons, guavas, pawpaws, avocado pears, custard-apples, and loquats are cultivated with great success. There are native fruits such as the Cape gooseberry, granadilla (fruit of the passion-vine), and *itungulu*, an acid plum which is much used for preserves. Apples and quinces thrive on higher land, towards the north of the colony. The staple production is Indian corn, of which two crops can be raised during the year with a little painstaking. This is the principal native food. The Zulus, however, raise sweet potatoes and beans to a large extent. Wheat and other cereals do better inland, but not so well as in Australia; hence the importation of flour from that country.

Of the various colonial enterprises, that of sugar culture stands at the head, the plantations extending the whole length of the country. Mills are in operation and sugar of the best quality is manufactured. The Natal Central Sugar Company's manufactory at Mount Edgecomb is the largest, having one hundred Indian coolies employed at the mill, besides nine hundred other laborers, natives and coolies, on the farm connected with the establishment.

Professor Maury predicted that Natal would prove a good locality for the cultivation of cotton, but his prediction has not been realized. Every attempt to raise it has proved a failure. Coffee for a time seemed to succeed, but tea is now taking its place, the soil in many localities being especially adapted for this plant. The largest tea estate at Kearsney has over two hundred acres under cultivation. The yield in 1887 was not far from eighty thousand pounds. A competent judge says: —

"No enterprise promises such a fair return upon capital invested, no occupation is surrounded with greater attractions. It is at once cleanly and interesting, and offers scope to the inventive and mechanical energies of those engaged therein."

The chief industry in the upland districts is that of cattle and sheep farming. On the coast, animals are severely bitten by ticks which come from the grass. The tetse fly is not found in Natal, but it is no uncommon thing to see a cow or horse covered with ticks, which, when filled with blood, are the size of a large pea. The ears of the poor animals are much affected. All that can be done is to rub on tar and grease or carbolic acid and oil. One species of tick adheres so firmly to the skin that it has to be removed by the application of sharp scissors. There is a smaller kind of tick, not larger than the head of a pin, which human beings have to encounter. It burrows in the flesh, producing sensations anything but agreeable. "Natal sores," which require ointments for healing and sometimes poultices, are the result of the bite, especially with persons not acclimated. When these little, almost invisible, insects get between the fingers, but particularly the toes, the irritation for a time is almost unbearable. Clergymen, when preaching, if thus disturbed, are sometimes obliged to curtail their sermons!

Pleuro-pneumonia, or lung sickness, which has swept away thousands, yea, hundreds of thousands of cattle, is continually breaking out in South Africa, inflicting serious loss upon the farmers. As there are few fences, it is next to impossible to keep diseased cattle in quarantine as in this country, and thus "stamp out" the disease. The method adopted to save enough oxen for necessary work, and cows for milk, is to inoculate them. Some resort to drenching the healthy cattle; that is, pouring down their throats two or three quarts of water in which is some of the virus of a diseased lung. This is to prevent contagion. But the majority of farmers prefer to make an incision in the lower part of the animal's tail and place there a seton with a few drops of the virus. If it "takes" violently, the tail swells and becomes a mass of putrefaction, and is then chopped off, and if it rises again the process is repeated. The unfortunate brutes suffer greatly in warm weather for want of something with which to brush off the flies.

Zulu cows are not noted for giving milk. It takes as many as six of the average kind to give as much as one good American cow. And they have this peculiarity, that they will not let the milker have any until the calves have first been fed. The milkman has to dispute with the calf as to who shall have the largest portion. And in case the calf dies, its mother refuses to give down her milk altogether. We have tried to teach African cows better manners, but all in vain. The horns of both oxen and cows are large and wide-spreading, very unlike those in New England.

There is another species of African pest, which, though it does not, like the tick, attack persons and animals, makes raids on food, clothing, books, and furniture. I refer to the ants. The ant kingdom is an exceedingly interesting one, an excellent description of which can be found in Professor Drummond's Tropical Africa. These ants, especially annoying to housewives, are of a brownish color; they build their nests in the walls or under floors, and forage in every direction, making the pantry their favorite resort. Black ants often build their nest in a tree, and woe be to the man who climbs it! Baldwin, the hunter, tells us of his ascending a tree overhanging a river, in order to shoot a sea cow, and says: "But the ants fell upon me so vigorously and in such countless numbers, biting so severely, that flesh and blood could not possibly hold out another second, and I was forced to descend. An old sea cow is indebted to the black ants for her life."

The termites or white ants are the most destructive, though, properly speaking, they are not ants at all — " holding an intermediate position between the orthopterous and hymenopterous families." They work out of sight, incessantly and indefatigably, forming galleries of hardened clay which ramify in various directions from the cell or nest of their king and queen. They have a partiality for the floors of dwelling houses, coming up through them into boxes or trunks, not lined with tin, converting their contents, however valuable, into a state of pulp. They often give human beings an unwelcome invitation to descend to a level with themselves. Walking one day in the parlor of a brother missionary, the floor suddenly gave way, and I sank three or four feet. On examination, I found that the ants had consumed, not only the sleepers, but the boards, rendering them too thin to support my weight. They often attack books, eating the margin as far as the print, at which they stop. "In many parts of Africa," Professor Drummond remarks, "I believe if a man lay down to sleep with wooden leg, it would be a heap of sawdust in the morning." Dr. Livingstone wrote of them: "At some of their operations they beat time in a curious manner. Hundreds of them are engaged in building a large tube, and they wish to beat it smooth. At a signal, they all give three or four energetic beats on the plaster in unison. It produces a sound like the dropping of rain off a bush when touched." The doctor regarded them as a blessing to South Africa, as agents employed in forming a fertile soil.[1]

It is interesting to observe the swarming process; so thick are they, and so white their wings, they have not inaptly been compared to "snowflakes floating about in the air." Cats, dogs, and fowls devour them eagerly. The natives also gather and roast them for eating, regarding them as a luxury. Dr. Livingstone once gave a chief a bottle of preserved apricots, and asked if he had ever tasted anything nicer; his reply was: "Yes: white ants!"

In some localities ant heaps rise to the height of seven or eight feet. Traveling one winter in the Orange Free State, where there was no firewood, I was in a quandary as to how I should get the wherewithal to boil my kettle. It occurred to me that I might utilize an ant heap near my wagon. Taking a spade, I cut off the apex of the conical mound, made a fireplace at the base, punched a hole from top to bottom for

[1] Livingstone's Researches in South Africa.

a flue, kindled a fire with some newspapers, and soon had a fine stove though of a novel character. On the top I placed the kettle, which soon boiled, after which the natives who accompanied me cooked their food.

The termites, not fancying the heat, ran in every direction. When bedtime came, all the natives had to do was to spread their mats on the ground by the side of a beautiful fire, which lasted till morning, thus sleeping with unusual comfort. As is their custom when any ingenious device is resorted to by white people, baffling their own skill, they broke out next morning with the expression: "*Yek' abelungu, ba hlulwa 'kufa kodwa* (O white men, nothing conquers you but death)!"

I am not aware that any contrivance for the extermination or extinction of the white ants has proved successful. Tar, arsenic, strychnine, corrosive sublimate, and kerosene have been tried, but in vain. The best remedy for the time being I found was hot ashes. Taking up the planks of a floor which the ants had begun to devour, and removing their champings, I sprinkled ashes freely about, which, clogging their mandibles, caused them to leave in disgust; but only to renew operations in another place.

The greatest curiosity connected with the termites is the queen, which attains the size and length of a man's finger, and resembles a mass of white jelly. Professor Drummond says: "She is two or three inches in length; in shape like a sausage, and white like a bolster." Her palace, or nest, is near the center of the heap, varying in size, but ordinarily just large enough to accommodate her majesty and the king, who is the size of an ordinary ant. No mason's trowel could make the sides of her abode smoother or neater than is done by the workers in the ant colony. In her cell she must remain, for the place of egress and ingress is only large enough to accommodate the common ant, and when she has laid a countless number of eggs she must die. It has been said that when she dies, or is removed, — like bees when their queen is destroyed, — the ants remove to another place; but I have been unable to verify this.

The great enemy of the termites is the ant-bear, an animal as large as a good-sized wolf, with a long nose, but a much longer tongue. It burrows into an ant heap, and puts out its tongue, upon which the insects creep unconscious of danger. When well covered, the tongue is drawn in, and the process is repeated until the hunger of the animal is appeased. Ant-bear holes are so common in South Africa that horseback riders have to use great caution lest they fall into them.

A Street in Durban, the Seaport Town of Natal.

CHAPTER XXX.

PHYSICAL FEATURES AND POLITICAL AFFAIRS.

DURBAN is the seaport town of Natal, and has a population, including natives and Asiatics, of nearly 30,000. Its large and substantial buildings, especially the town hall, which cost about £50,000, would be an ornament to any English or American city. Its surroundings are exceedingly picturesque. On the "Berea," an elevation in the suburbs, reached by tram cars, are numerous and tasteful cottages which command a fine view of the lighthouse and outer anchorage. Its botanical garden, well stocked with flowers, plants, and trees, exotic and indigenous, and under the supervision of a scientific curator, is a favorite place of resort. The streets are wide, hard, and kept scrupulously clean. Water is at present brought from a small stream a short distance from the town, but a scheme is projected for conveying a larger supply from a river ten miles away at an expense of £30,000. The matter of defense is not overlooked. A battery, to be furnished with guns of the latest model, commanding the entrance to the bay, is in process of construction.

As Durban is one of the principal gateways to the Transvaal, the El Dorado in South Africa, it has before it the brightest prospects, and bids fair to become a second Melbourne or San Francisco. There seems no reason why it should not be a coaling station for steamers from America to China by way of the Cape of Good Hope, as well as from England to Australia.

In point of religious and literary privileges the town is highly favored, having large and commodious churches, able ministers, a public library, reading room, and two daily newspapers. The Natal Mercury, an old and popular paper, has for its chief editor a gentleman of great ability, Sir John Robinson, who has lately received the honor of knighthood. His love and labors for the good of his adopted country prove him to be a Natalian of the right stamp. With untiring patience he has "dinned into the colonial ears for the last quarter of a century" their need of responsible government. May he live to see this boon secured! A keen observer has justly remarked, "The three-cornered South African problem is no longer Blacks, Boers, and British, but Republicanism, Responsible Colonialism, and Crown Colonialism. Until Natal strikes for freedom and gains a voice in the direction of its own affairs, it will be behind in the great northern race."

The Natalians have voted, with a small majority however, to ask the home government for the privilege of ruling themselves. But the question has not yet been decided. Evidently expecting it, the progressive party, with

Sir John Robinson at their head, have drafted a new responsible constitution for the colony and presented it to the Legislative Council. Among the things recommended, I am glad to see that an annual grant of £20,000 has been devoted to "raise the natives in the scale of civilization."

Maritzburg, the colonial capital, fifty miles from Durban, with which it is connected by rail, has been called the loveliest of South African towns. I think it deserves that appellation. Its streets are lined with tall Australian gums, which answer the twofold purpose of shade and lightning conductors. Good drinking water is brought in aqueducts from a fountain in the suburbs. Fort Napier, on an elevation just outside, commands the city and surroundings. Prominent among buildings are the legislative hall, hospital, and the residence of the governor. In the center is an immense square for market purposes, at the end of which is a neat granite monument commemorative of colonists who fell in the Zulu war. Opposite the legislative hall stands a fine statue of Queen Victoria, also a bust of Sir Bartle Frere, a statesman whose memory is cherished with profound respect by all Natalians. The scenery about the capital is exceedingly beautiful, and on the road leading to the coast the traveler, if he has been in Switzerland, is often reminded of that country. Lofty cliffs and huge rocks give variety to the view. In some parts of the colony are seen immense slabs of granite on hillsides, apparently just ready to launch into deep ravines below, the earth having been washed away from underneath. One, near Esidumbini, measures one hundred feet in length, ninety in width, and thirty in thickness. A cave underneath served as a hiding place for Zulus in the time of Chaka.

No thorough geological survey of Natal has been made as yet. A few years ago, there appeared in The Natal Journal the following brief, but good, description : —

" The country is composed of granite, gneiss, trap, sandstone, and shale. Of sandstone there are two kinds, the old coarse species, which forms the summits of the Table Mountains, and a much finer grained sort which is associated with carboniferous strata containing impressions of vegetable remains imbedded in the layers. The trap is of different ages. The shale is sometimes gray and sometimes red, and is fissured and laminated. Enormous masses of trap rock are scattered over the face of the country. The bed of every water course is encumbered with them. The granite hills inland are generally broad, low, and smoothly rounded protrusions. These are square, tabular elevations, molded entirely of trap, and may be at once distinguished by the eye from the true sandstone-slabbed Table Mountains, notwithstanding their general resemblance. There is abundant evidence that during past centuries volcanic eruptions have had much to do in mingling together in a most confused manner various kinds of rocks in every part of the colony."

A few gold mines are worked both in Natal and Zululand, but none have as yet proved as rich as those in the Transvaal. But beds of good coal are extensive in the upper districts, and are destined greatly to enrich the colony. Steamers plying between Durban and London are using it instead of English coal, and South America is applying to the colonial government for a monthly supply.

The flora of Natal presents much that is attractive and beautiful and well worth attention. During the rainy season the country is brilliant with flowers, and even when the rains have ceased many more quiet but interesting plants may be found. Perhaps no orders are more fully represented than the *Leguminosæ* and *Compositæ*. Examples of the former are the Kaffir boom, with its showy scarlet blossoms and bright red seeds with the black spot around the hilum, used by natives and white children alike for necklaces. Throughout the colony can be found the acacias. An Australian species has been introduced and is extensively cultivated for the bark, which is sent to England for tanning purposes.

Among the *Compositæ*, those which are better known than the others are the everlastings or immortelles, the pink and yellow being very common, while the silvery-white variety, with the delicate pink tinge around the disk, is found in the upper districts. One species of *nym-*

phœa, the blue water lily, is quite numerous. The arum, erroneously called calla in America, is found in almost every marshy place.

The beautiful blue and white agapanthus, the graceful littonia, and sandersonia, and the aloes are among the members of the lily family. Many of the so-called lilies in Natal belong to the order *amaryllidaceæ;* as, for example, the "Natal lily," with its pink-veined perianth, and the "fire lily," whose showy scarlet bells contrast vividly with the blackness of the hills after the annual burning of the grass.

A few epiphytic, and numerous terrestrial, orchids are found in Natal. Some are showy and conspicuous, while others are dull and hardly distinguishable from the grass. Among the cycads, the stangeria is a beautiful form, with its long, frond-like leaves and central cone. Grasses and sedges abound, and the lover of ferns would have no lack of material for investigation.

Palms and wild bananas and the ungainly euphorbias are conspicuous among the larger plants.

The trees used for cabinetwork are yellow-wood (*podocarpus*); sneezewood (*pteroxylon utile*); stinkwood (*oreodaphne bullata*), so called for its odor, which, however, is useful, in that worms do not attack it; black ironwood (*olea laurifolia*), a hard, solid wood which takes a fine polish; and many others of which more use could be made than has been yet attempted.

Physical Features. 289

Waterfalls in Natal are common and beautiful. From numerous fountains in the hillsides there issue streams which roll down till they unite with rivers winding their way to the Indian Ocean. A perpendicular fall of three hundred and sixty feet on the Umgeni River is one of surpassing beauty. A Dutch farmer, in attempting to cross the ford about a hundred yards above, in an ox-wagon, had a most narrow escape. His "forelooper" (ox leader), a Zulu lad of sixteen years, could not swim, and was told by his master to get into the wagon. The Dutchman knew his oxen well — had often seen them swim through swollen streams, and believed he could trust them in this instance. Alas! he had not calculated on the rapidity of the current. The oxen could not reach the opposite landing, and to his horror he found that bullocks, wagon, and all were approaching the rapids. The native, losing his presence of mind, plunged into the river and was soon taken over the fall. The Dutchman, made of different stuff, concluded that so long as there was life there was hope, and made a desperate attempt to save himself. He cracked his long whip most energetically, calling on each ox by name to do his best. The brave fellows, inspired doubtless by the frantic cries of their driver, swam for dear life. The two leaders got a foothold on the bank, and just as the wagon swung about, within a few feet of the abyss, the faithful beasts drew it out and up to a place of safety.

The political affairs of Natal are administered

by a governor, appointed by the crown, aided by an executive and legislative council, composed of thirty members, who retain their seat for four years. The administration of justice is conducted by a supreme court, by courts of magistrates in various counties, also by circuit courts held when required. A special judge is appointed for cases among the natives, who are allowed the privilege of appeal to a higher court. Should the matter in dispute be of the value of five hundred pounds, an appeal can be made to the privy council in England.

Natives, on certain conditions, may come out from under native law and be governed precisely as white men. Few, however, seem disposed to avail themselves of this privilege. Doubtless the reason is that under purely English law they would not be allowed to exchange cattle for women and practice polygamy. Those who conform to English customs and dwell in furnished houses of European construction are exempt from the annual hut tax. The great mass prefer to live, as did their fathers, in Zulu style.

As respects ecclesiastical affairs in Natal, the largest denomination is that of Wesleyan Methodists, but Presbyterians, Congregationalists, Episcopalians (Church of England), and Roman Catholics are well represented. There are two Baptist churches and one Jewish synagogue.

Colonial education is under the direction of a council, composed of ten members, with two superintendents, one for the European, the

UMZINYATI WATERFALL, INANDA, NATAL.

other for the native, schools. There are several collegiate institutions which compare favorably with those in other countries.

Natal's exports are sugar, wool, hides, horns, tallow, arrowroot, ginger, cayenne pepper, tea, ivory (from the interior), and the bark of an acacia tree, useful for tanning purposes.

Imports are chiefly timber, furniture, agricultural implements, leather manufactures, carriages of various descriptions, clothing, groceries, ironmongery, machinery, ardent spirits, etc.

The revenue is derived principally from the customs charges, auction dues, duty on firearms, sale of stamps, gunpowder, crown lands, taxation of Europeans and natives, transfer dues, excise, post offices, licenses, etc.

The native hut tax amounts in the aggregate to £75,000 per annum, and the custom dues on blankets and beads, purchased to a large extent by natives, reach the sum of £15,000. The following comparative statement of the value of imports and exports and customs receipts for the years 1888 and 1889 shows the rate of progress: —

IMPORTS.	1889.	1888.
Value of imports	£4,527,015 0 0	£2,890,468 0 0
Customs revenue	369,089 3 1	290,084 8 1

EXPORTS.		
Colonial	£957,132 0 0	£941,562 0 0
Non-Colonial	¹699,186 0 0	¹476,309 0 0
Total exports	£1,656.318 0 0	£1,417,871 0 0

¹ These figures include rough gold to the value of £584,933 0 0   £391,643 0 0

According to a late estimate, the combined trade of the colony for 1889 was not far short of six millions sterling.

Railways are being pushed with rapidity both to the Transvaal and Orange Free State. The Grand Trunk Line has reached Charleston, on the border of the Transvaal, only one hundred and thirty miles from Johannesburg, the greatest "mushroom city" in Africa. This railway is said to be "unequaled in English colonies for profit." It increased the past year to such an extent that, according to a published estimate, after paying all expenses, a sum of one hundred thousand pounds would accrue to the general revenue of the colony.

Various industries now occupy the attention of Natalians, besides the cultivation of tea and sugar cane. Some are engaged in ostrich farming, a few in raising ground nuts (peanuts) for the oil. One farmer obtained three hundred bushels from a single acre.

Sericulture is attracting attention, the government affording a little aid. Queens and eggs are imported from Italy. The mulberry grows finely, and there appears no reason why this industry should not prove a success. The most lucrative business in the upper districts is sheep farming. It is said that a man with a moderate capital invested in land and sheep is pretty sure to obtain a good return.

With the influx of the Anglo-Saxon race into South Africa, the native question is one of deep interest. Zulus in the service of Europeans are generally obedient and peaceful, but the influence of their hereditary chiefs is great. Should any real or supposed wrong lead those chiefs to combine against the whites, the result would be war and bloodshed. Let us hope and pray for better things. Instead of believing that they are "doomed like the redskins to fade away before the fiercer energy and tougher fiber and the higher mental power of their pale brethren," as Hepworth Dixon predicted would be the case with the blacks in our southern states, we cherish the belief that they will improve under the just and benign authority of England, and, living peacefully alongside of the superior race, will rise gradually but surely to a high standard of Christianity and civilization. If in the course of divine providence this occurs, it will be, as Froude the historian observed, the "solution of a problem worth more than all the diamonds of Kimberly."

APPENDIX.

LATER MISSIONS.

FROM latest statistics, the Gordon Memorial Mission in Natal (Scotch), in charge of Rev. James Dalzell, M.D., and his wife, is in a prosperous condition. This mission was founded in 1868 by the Countess of Aberdeen, to commemorate the purpose of her son, the late Honorable James H. H. Gordon, to devote his life to mission work in South Africa, a purpose not executed owing to his early death. A farm was purchased in the upper part of Natal, which is thickly populated by natives, and Dr. Dalzell, with his zealous wife, is here laboring most successfully. Church members in full standing, April, 1890, were 113. Number of pupils in the schools connected with the station, 322.

Two sisters of Mrs. Dalzell, the Misses Lorimer, have a Zulu Girls' Home, to which their services are given gratuitously. The late Dr. Somerville, "the world's evangelist," in his visit to South Africa visited this station and spoke of it in the highest terms.

At Impolweni the Free Church of Scotland has an interesting mission in charge of Rev. James Scott, with a church membership of 163, and two schools, with 122 pupils. There are five branch stations connected with Impolweni. Also at Maritzburg there is a flourishing native church under the superintendence of Rev. Mr. Bruce.

The Hanoverian (German) Society has, according to latest reports, in Natal and Zululand: —

Missionaries, white,	25
Native helpers,	50
Stations,	22
Church members,	1,782

Church of the Province of South Africa (English Episcopal): —

Ordained laborers, white,	5
Ordained laborers, native,	3
Lay laborers, white,	4
Lay laborers, native,	18
Lady assistants, white,	3
Stations,	12
Baptized Zulus,	1,644

Its chief centers of labor are Durban and Maritzburg.

The superintendent of native missions in Natal, Rev. A. Ikin, D.D. (Church of England), reports: —

Native converts,	475
Stations for Sunday services,	16
Night schools,	8
Day schools,	5
White evangelists,	3
Native evangelists,	23

The Swedish (Lutheran) Church has three missionaries laboring in Natal and Zululand, and not without success.

THE ZULU LANGUAGE.

One peculiarity of the Zulu language is the *clicks* derived from intercourse with the Hottentots. They are what are called dental, palatal, and lateral, owing to the manner in which they are spoken. The dental is made by compressing the tip of the tongue between the teeth and hastily drawing it back. The letter *c* is used to denote it. The palatal is a cracking sound which the tongue makes in the roof of the mouth, and is represented by the letter *q*. The lateral is a sound like clucking to a horse, caused by the tongue and double teeth united. The letter *x* represents it. Dr. Lepsius in his Standard Alphabet suggested characters for these clicks, but missionaries in Zululand are not inclined to adopt them. The letters used for them are always in italics.

Appendix. 297

There is another sound in the language, happily occurring only in a few words, pronounced as a guttural from the bottom of the throat. It is not a click, but, according to a philologist, " a peculiar, hard, rough sound that seems to be made by contracting the throat and giving the breath a forcible expulsion, at the same time modifying the sound with a tremulous motion of the epiglottis." Only Zulus, and whites born among them, can express it.

Each class of nouns has a prefix which undergoes a change in forming the plural from the singular. In one class the prefix is *um*, which in the plural is changed into *aba;* for instance, *umuntu* (person), *abantu* (persons). Another class has the prefix *in*, which in the plural is changed to *izin;* for example, *inkomo* (cow), *izinkomo* (cows). In still another class, *ili* is changed to *ama*, as *ilizwi* (word), *amazwi* (words). The possessive is formed in a singular manner. Each class of nouns having its preformative letter, that letter is used in forming this case, *w* standing for nouns beginning with *u* in the singular, and *b* for the plural. Thus *ami* (of me) *umfana* (boy), becomes in the possessive *umfana wami* (my boy); plural *aba*, *abafana bami* (my boys). In another class, *in* being the prefix in the singular, *y* is used, making *yami*, in the plural, *zami;* thus, *inkomo yami* (my cow), *izinkomo zami* (my cows). In forming the possessive *his* or *her*, the basis is *a* (of) and *ke* (him). For example, in the class commencing with *um*, we have *umfana wake* (his boy), plural *abafana bake* (his boys). With *in* for prefix, *y* is used, as *inkomo yake* (his cow), plural, *izinkomo zake* (his cows). For the possessive *their*, the ground form is *abo:* for example, *abantwana babo* (their children), *izinkomo zabo* (their cows).

Great simplicity is apparent in the construction of verbs. Take, for example, the verb love, *ukutanda*, *uku* being the sign of the infinitive, and *tanda* the root. *Ngi* is the pronoun of the first person, and *ya* the auxiliary. *Ngi ya tanda* (I love); second person, *u ya tanda* (thou lovest); third person, *u ya tanda* (he loves); plural, *si ya tanda* (we love); *ni ya tanda* (ye love); *ba ya tanda* (they love). Imperfect tense, *nga tanda* (I was loving); *wa tanda* (thou wast loving); *wa tanda* (he was loving). Perfect tense, *ngi tandile* (I have loved); *u tandile* (thou hast loved); etc. Pluperfect, *bengi tandile* (I had loved); *u be tandile* (thou hadst loved); etc. Future, *ngi ya ku tanda* (I will love); *u ya ku tanda* (thou wilt love); etc. The imperative is the root, *tanda*.

Rev. Lewis Grout, for fifteen years a missionary in Natal, author of a Zulu grammar and a book entitled "Zululand," justly remarks in regard to the verbs: "One root will often give us a large stem with a good number of branches and no small amount of fruit. Thus from the verb *bona*, see, we have *bonisa*, cause to see; *bonisisa*, show, show clearly; *bonela*, see for; *bonelela*, see for each other; *bonisana*, cause each other to see, show each other; *bonakala*, appear, be visible; *bonakalisa*, make visible; *umboneli*, a spectator; *umbonelo*, a spectacle; *umbonisi*, an overseer; *umboniso*, a show; *isibono*, a sight, curiosity; *isiboniso*, a vision; *isibonakalo*, an appearance; *isibonakaliso*, a revelation; and all this without going into the passive voice; as *bonwa*, be seen; *bonisiwa*, caused to be seen; *bonisiswa*, cause to be clearly seen; et cetera."

THE EXILED CHIEFS.

Mr. Melmoth Osborn, C.M.G., British commissioner and chief magistrate in Zululand, attributes the late political revolution, which rendered the expatriation of the Zulu chiefs necessary, to the intrigues of Dutch farmers who had settled in the country. "The Boers," he says, "assisted the Usutus to expel Usibepu, causing frightful bloodshed, and then quarreled with their allies in regard to the division of the land. The Boers, in truth, ran all over the country and respected no man's rights. They poisoned the minds of the Zulus against us by inciting them to rebellion. What they said was simply this: 'We [the Boers] made Mpande king over you. He ruled you as an independent sovereign and lived and reigned to a good old age. Now the British have taken your country and deposed your king. This would not have happened had you stuck to us,' etc. The Boers indeed proclaimed Dinizulu king on the death of Cetywayo, and intrigued with Ndabuko (Dinizulu's uncle and Cetywayo's full brother) to oust the British from Zululand. Lucas Meyer and his colleagues even went so far as to perform the scriptural ceremony of anointing Dinizulu, and they encouraged him to ride about on a white horse, and to flout British authority in every way possible. I should remark that pensions had been granted to the principal chiefs to compensate them for the loss of any advantages attaching to their position. These were refused by Dinizulu and his uncle, Ndabuko, who was the principal and most dangerous offender. In consequence of the dispute between the Boers and Ndabuko over the division of the land, Sir Arthur Havelock, as special commissioner, made an agreement with the Boer representatives, dated October 22, 1886, by which a certain line was drawn and the Boers were to be kept within the territory known as the New Republic. The Boers, however, did not respect the line of demarcation, and I, who was doing my best to preserve order and prevent injustice to the Zulus, proclaimed the country to be under British protection. Afterwards it was annexed to the British crown, and magistrates were appointed to administer justice and secure good order. The Zulus — the vast majority of them — were anxious to become British subjects; it was only the royal household and a small section of the people inflamed by the Boers, and those

Zulus that were included in the New Republic, who attempted to resist. The Boers said to the Zulus: 'Look at us; the British came and took our country, but we beat them and drove them out. Why don't you do the same?' Dinizulu asserted his supposed right to rule as an independent king. He even put people to death, and seized the cattle of others. The magistrates and officers of the government were ignored; communications were made direct to the special commissioner, Sir Arthur Havelock; and Dinizulu posed as an independent ruler, of whom the Queen was but the equal and no more. The country was in a very serious state, and I foresaw that worse trouble was impending. There was only one possible remedy. I consider it would be a disastrous mistake to allow the exiled chiefs to go back to Zululand. From the moment of their departure the country has been peaceful; but if they were permitted to return there would only be a repetition of what occurred after Cetywayo's restoration. There was fearful bloodshed, and misery to women and children, immediately after that event. Zululand is now as quiet and prosperous as any country on earth, and does not cost the British taxpayer a single penny for its internal administration. British rule is accepted by all the Zulus, as is evidenced by the hundreds of cases which they bring before the resident magistrates every month."

www.ingramcontent.com/pod-product-compliance
Lightning Source LLC
Chambersburg PA
CBHW030730230426
43667CB00007B/660